**Summary**

- THE ORIGINS
  OF THE MUSEUM
  PAGE **4**

- VICTOR HUGO
  PLACE ROYALE
  PAGE **12**

- TOUR
  SUMMARY
  PAGE **28**

- CHRONOLOGY
  PAGE **74**

- FAMILY TREE
  PAGE **78**

- PRACTICAL
  INFORMATION
  PAGE **79**

## The origins of the museum

On 21st June 1901, before the Paris city council, M. Froment-Meurice read out a letter from his uncle Paul Meurice:

*12th June 1901*

*To the City Councillors of Paris*
*Dear Sirs,*
*[...] I wish to give Paris the opportunity of providing France with the Maison de Victor Hugo [...]. We could [...] assemble over five hundred of his drawings there [...] and one entire room in the museum [...] would be decorated with bird, flower, chimaera and figure motifs, which the poet himself carved, chiselled and painted in the most charming and original manner.*
*[...] we could provide the museum with a collection of paintings and drawings inspired by his poems, novels and plays [...].*
*Lastly, Georges and Jeanne [...] will recreate, within the Maison de Victor Hugo, his bedroom in the avenue d'Eylau [...].*
*Now where is this Maison de Victor Hugo to be ?*
*It will be [...] in the home in Paris in which he spent the greatest number of years, from 1833 to 1848, the house of the Romantic period, where he wrote his epic dramas and fought his greatest battles, the house situated at n° 6, place Royale [...].*

In November of that same year, a celebration was planned in the place des Vosges to commemorate the centenary of Victor Hugo's birth.

This was part of a whole programme of events organised by the State in conjunction with the Ville de Paris, to take place between 25th February and 2nd March 1902.

At 10 a.m. on 26th February, the poet's birthday, all the major representatives of the political and administrative institutions and official bodies gathered in the Panthéon for the ceremony.

The same afternoon saw the unveiling of the monument carved by the sculptor Barrias, in the place Victor-Hugo[1].

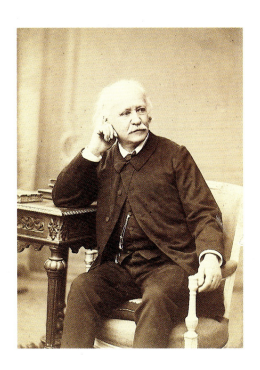

A. Gerschel
*Paul Meurice*

The consecration of the Maison de Victor Hugo, on Sunday 2nd March, was one of the highspots of the week's celebrations.

The inauguration of the museum had originally been planned to coincide with this event, but it was held up by problems involved in transferring the primary school still under lease in the Hôtel de Rohan-Guéménée. In the first instance, therefore, the museum was merely consecrated, and a great deal still had to be accomplished. It nevertheless provided the occasion for the council to organise a grand fête in the place des Vosges, which lasted throughout the afternoon and evening.

All eyes were drawn to the façade of the future museum, draped with flags and garlands of leaves, its dedication plaque, still visible today, in pride of place. The other plaque, commemorating the years Victor Hugo spent in the house, had been placed there in 1898. On the corner, a tall banner had been unfurled to mark the day's event.

The first part of the ceremony was a parade by school children, who strew palms and flowers before the cast of Victor Hugo, designed for a haut-relief by the sculptor Bareau.

The façade of the Hôtel Rohan-Guéménée
2nd March 1902

Charles Crespin
*Le Génie de la Renommée descendant sur la maison du poète, place des Vosges*
Cutting from
*Le Petit Parisien, Supplément littéraire illustré*
9th March 1902

Auguste Lepèr(e)
*Fête du centenaire, place des Vosges*
2nd March 190(2)

The second half, composed and conducted by Gustave Charpentier, was entitled *Apothéose de Victor Hugo*. The workers' Muse, embodied by Jeanne Girard, a typographer, was seen plucking the petals off a rose before Victor Hugo's statue, as the notes of Gustave Charpentier's song of apotheosis rang out.

Suddenly the square was illuminated. The titles of Victor Hugo's works were etched along the fences, an architectural decor of Oriental splendour was revealed. Finally the Maison de Victor Hugo became wreathed in light and a giant Muse with outspread wings was outlined, carrying a torch and palm.

On 30th June 1903, the inauguration of the Maison de Victor Hugo saw Paul Meurice's efforts finally rewarded.

Paul Meurice (1818-1905) was half-brother to the renowned goldsmith Froment-Meurice. He first met Victor Hugo when he was very young, through one of his friends at the Collège Charlemagne, Auguste Vacquerie (1819-1895). The latter, who was a fervent admirer of Victor Hugo, had got to know Victor Hugo in December 1835 and was a great friend of the family, who were living at that time in the place Royale. His brother Charles married Léopoldine Hugo in 1843. In 1836 Paul Meurice was invited to Victor Hugo's home and thus discovered the apartment he was to turn into a museum many years later. For almost fifty years, his affection and devotion to the poet never wavered.

In 1848, when Victor Hugo founded *L'Evénement*, Paul Meurice was appointed editor. The newspaper first lent its support to Louis Bonaparte as presidential candidate, and went on to defend democracy before being abolished following the coup d'Etat. An article by François-Victor Hugo led to the imprisonment of both men in September 1851. In 1869 Paul Meurice and the sons of Victor Hugo and Auguste Vacquerie jointly founded *Le Rappel*, to which he personally contributed a large number of articles.

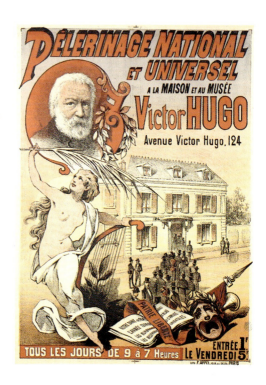

During the long period of exile which followed the coup d'Etat of 2nd December 1851, he remained in France, looking after Victor Hugo's affairs and getting his works published.

He wrote a number of plays and novels himself, collaborated with Dumas and also adapted *Les Misérables*, *Notre-Dame de Paris* and *Quatrevingt-treize* for the theatre.

In his literary testament, dated 23rd September 1875, Victor Hugo entrusted Paul Meurice, Auguste Vacquerie and Ernest Lefèvre with the publication of his manuscripts. Paul Meurice was therefore instrumental in the creation of a National Edition of his mentor's works.

It was his almost pious devotion to Victor Hugo which led to the opening of this museum in the place des Vosges, almost twenty years after the poet's death.

On 12th May 1889, the house in which Victor Hugo spent the last years of his life, at n° 124 avenue Victor-Hugo, was opened to the public. The interior, the living-room and bedroom in particular, were recreated as they had been in his lifetime; many mementoes of Victor Hugo and Juliette Drouet were displayed, some of which found their way to the present museum in the place des Vosges. The house only remained open for one year, however.

The mementoes owned by Paul Meurice formed the bedrock of the future museum in the place des Vosges. Drawing up the collections entailed commissioning a great many works between 1901 and 1902 : A. Besnard (*La Première d'Hernani*), E. Grasset (*Eviradnus*), L.-O. Merson (*Une larme pour une goutte d'eau*), J.-F. Raffaelli (*La Fête des 80 ans du poète*), G. Rochegrosse (*Les Burgraves*), A. Roll (*La Veillée sous l'Arc de Triomphe*), A. Steinlen (*Les Pauvres Gens*), D. Vierge (*Les Funérailles de Charles Hugo*), L.-A. Willette (*La Mort de Gavroche*)... The 1879 portrait of Victor Hugo by Bonnat, a copy of the one hanging in the Château de Versailles, was commissioned from the artist himself.

There were fewer commissions in the field of sculpture, but notable contributions included Auguste Rodin's bust of the poet and *L'Apothéose de Victor Hugo* by Henri Cros.

These commissions, designed to illustrate Victor Hugo's works, represented an original aspect in the museum's creation, complemented by a great many purchases, sometimes made directly by Paul Meurice from the artists themselves. Victor Hugo's portrait by F.-N. Chifflart was one of these.

A number of donations were also made to Paul Meurice, including the portrait of Victor Hugo's maternal grandparents and the portrait of Sophie Trébuchet.

Paul Meurice's collection was complemented by the collection of Juliette Drouet's nephew, Louis Koch. This included the furniture designed by Victor Hugo for Hauteville Fairy, Juliette Drouet's house in Guernsey, the decorative elements and panels painted by the poet for the Chinese drawing-room at Hauteville Fairy, approximately 250 pottery items, a significant collection of drawings by Victor Hugo, a great many mementoes (including the table from *La Légende des siècles* and the quill pens from *Les Misérables*...), drawings, engravings and photographs...

The collection bequeathed by Paul Beuve also played a part in the museum's creation. It covered all the popular imagery, knick-knacks and objects which commercial interest and the cult of Victor Hugo could conceivably inspire : pipe bowls, tobacco pots, plates, firedogs, bottles, insignia, calendars, miscellaneous advertisements...

Another key contribution was the donation granted to the Ville de Paris by the poet's grandchildren, Georges and Jeanne, who recreated specifically for the museum their grandfather's bedroom in the avenue d'Eylau.

Reconstituting the Chinese drawing-room played an important part in the proceedings. Hanging the panels and adapting them to a museum environment was not without its problems and a number of alterations proved to be necessary. This is quite clear when one compares the room's present aspect with contemporary photographs taken in Juliette Drouet's house. The walls had to be panelled and racks made to accommodate the plates..., to complete the overall effect a few items of pottery were added to the ones already destined for the specifically-designed racks, recalling the original appearance of the room.

The museum was inaugurated with much solemnity on 30th June 1903.

The layout was far less extensive than it is today and has since been totally altered.

The tour began on the first floor with a room containing drawings of Victor Hugo's works. One then entered the vast room housing the paintings, Paul Meurice's commissions (including Bonnat's portrait) and the bust by David d'Angers. The library came next.

On the second floor, the antechamber led to a room devoted to Victor Hugo's drawings, now the red drawing-room. *Le Burg à la Croix* hung here, together with the two lighthouse drawings. The following room was the Chinese drawing-room, which is still in the same place today.

Reconstitution of Victor Hugo's bedroom, avenue d'Eylau

The visit ended with a small annexe containing more drawings and the faithfully recreated bedroom of the avenue d'Eylau.

Despite a note of discord struck by an article deploring the lack of warmth and emotion derived from the presentation of the writer's personal memorabilia[2], the press welcomed the new museum in enthusiastic terms : [...] *the Paris council now owns an admirably designed, comprehensive, not to say impressive monument, erected in a spirit of piety and gratitude by a noble city to a noble poet*[3]. The articles recall the generosity of the museum's benefactor, dwell on the commissions by contemporary artists and on Victor Hugo's own drawings... And in the eulegistic and characteristically exaggerated terms so often used of Victor Hugo by his contemporaries, a number of journalists even qualified the new museum as a sanctuary. A single example will suffice : *For the thinker, therefore, a visit to the house represents a veritable pilgrimage; these walls will soon become a virtual shrine, perpetuating in the most material, tangible, living fashion the memory of a much-loved poet, considered not only as the greatest of the great, but also as the most charitable, sympathetic, gentle and best of men...*[4]

1. This monument was melted down in 1941 and can therefore only be seen in photographs. The bas-reliefs are on display in Calais, at the Musée des Beaux-Arts et de la Dentelle and also in the town park at Veules-les-Roses.
2. Article by Jules de Saint-Hilaire in *Le Journal des Arts*, 3rd February 1904.
3. Article by Camille Gronkowski, *Le Gaulois du Dimanche, Supplément Hebdomadaire Littéraire et illustré*, 27th-28th June 1903.
4. Article by L. Méaulle, *Le Monde illustré*, 27th June 1903, p. 620.

# Victor Hugo place Royale

The mansion in which Victor Hugo lived, commonly known as the Hôtel de Rohan-Guéménée, was built by Isaac Arnauld, King's counsellor and administrator of Finances, who was granted the land in June 1605 when the Parc des Tournelles was made into allotments. The house was passed on to the marquess of Lavardin (1612-1621), and then to Pierre Jacquet, seigneur de Tigery (1621-1639), before becoming the property of Louis de Rohan, prince of Guéménée, in whose illustrious family it remained until 1784. Significant improvements were made to the interior but bankruptcy forced the family to sell up, and the house was bought by Jacques Desmary. In 1785 he was given permission to build two balconies, one on the first floor and the other on the second, neither of which remain today.

In 1797, the mansion became the property of the Péan de Saint-Gilles family, whose descendants bequeathed it in 1873 to the Ville de Paris. A school then occupied the premises.

Victor Hugo moved into the place Royale on 25th October 1832, during rehearsals of his play *Le Roi s'amuse*[1]. The riot, which erupted in June 1832 during General Lamarque's funeral, made him decide to leave his home at 9, rue Jean-Goujon, where he had been living since May 1830, so that he could be nearer the centre of Paris and some of his friends, such as Charles Nodier, librarian at the Arsenal, and Théophile Gautier, who lived with his parents at 8, place Royale until 1834.

The lease was signed on 12th July 1832 for a three, six or nine-year term beginning 1st January 1833, and the description was of *a second-floor apartment overlooking the Place Royale, with a wing in a house situated at n° 6 Place Royale, Paris; the said apartment is composed on the street side of an antechamber, dining-room and drawing-room, with a kitchen overlooking the courtyard, several rooms in a wing reached by a corridor, with an exit via a small staircase, conveniences, woodshed, three servants' rooms and a cellar*. The annual rent was 1500 Francs, to be paid every quarter in equal sums, as of 1st April 1833.

These changes are reflected in the family's letters. On 30th October 1832, Léopoldine, the poet's elder daughter, aged eight at the time, wrote to her friend Louise Bertin : *I do beg your parden for not replying erlier but we mooved to place Royale n° [6] we are very nicely set up here. we have a lovely balcony over the place Royale I really am sorry not to have written before its not my fault its because Father had to orgenize all his paintings and that takes a long time [...] I get very bored Ive no frends here Its too far away and I cannot see them ofen as in the rue jean-goujon*.

The same day, Victor Hugo also wrote to Louise Bertin : *I want you to feel sorry for me [...] involved as I have been for the past week in the ghastly upheaval of moving house, with the help of those so-called convenient machines which led so many poor devils to move in a body to their final abode during the cholera plague. I have been in this state of utter chaos for a week now, planting nails and hammering, and looking for all the world like a robber. It is an appalling experience.*

Victor Hugo found himself criticised by some for moving so far away. On 9th June 1834, for instance, Gaspard de Pons wrote : *I may even ask you to lunch or dinner, because [...] we are now so far apart that it seems the only way of ensuring we meet, since you have devised this extraordinary notion of settling in the Marais [...]. So farewell, my lord of the marshes\* [...]*[2].

The mansion was made up of a main building on the square, with two wings at right angles, each with ten façade casement windows overlooking the courtyard. The latter was surrounded by stables and outhouses and communicated with the impasse Guéménée. The left wing formed a

---

\* *Translator's note* : «Marais» in French signifies marsh, hence the pun.

The fountain in the garden at Hauteville House

mezzanine on the garden. Victor Hugo did not in fact have a stable, as he did not own a carriage. The top floor housed the servants' quarters and attics.

In the garden was a vase-shaped fountain which Victor Hugo bought in August 1847 and took with him into exile. It can still be seen in the garden of Hauteville House in Guernsey. *This fountain has had a strange destiny. Its reflection used to ripple over a freshwater pool surrounded by tritons and nymphs bathing their marble limbs, in the centre of a beautiful garden in the place Royale [...]. Today, on a worn granite foundation, it stands overlooking the sea in a foreign land. [...] This monument to the past weeps unceasingly over the present, with the Ocean as fathomless well and the storm for reservoir*[3].

Efforts to reconstitute the house as it was in those days are hampered by the alterations carried out in the 1860s and the limited number of objects and mementoes. We do, however, have access to documents which give a fairly accurate idea of the house as it was. Victor Hugo's polisher, *Guigon aîné demeurant rue des Tournelles 24*, kept a detailed logbook, which is still preserved in the museum, of all the jobs he carried out between November 1836 and April 1844. Guigon waxed and treated the floors, but was equally responsible for taking up and beating the carpets every summer and looking after the furniture. He also took on the rôle of upholsterer, hanging curtains, drapes and tapestries, fixing paintings and frames... His logbook is crammed with references to the Hugo family and gives a valuable insight into their lifestyle. Other clues are given through the accounts kept by Victor Hugo and Adèle, bills from suppliers, reports on the work carried out by painters, carpenters, upholsterers and locksmiths and even notes from the heating engineer and plumber.

Contemporary accounts also provide vital clues to the layout of the rooms and the furniture, as demonstrated in the descriptions given by Vassili Petrovitch Botkine, who visited Victor Hugo on 27th July 1835[4], and Gustave Masson[5] and Eugène Woestyn[6], who called on him in 1839 and 1846 respectively.

The apartment must have measured approximately 280 m². Archive material would suggest that the kitchen, with one window overeooking the courtyard, has since been replaced by part of the staircase. In Victor Hugo's day, the staircase must therefore have been nearer the building known today as 6 bis. This hypothesis is given credence by the number of windows overlooking the courtyard, and also goes to explain the curious presence of these false openings one can see today in the staircase, one of which would appear to correspond to the front door and the other to the door which used to lead from the antechamber to the kitchen.

The poet left his mark on the house. It was an emporium of paintings and frames, including drawings by L. Boulanger, C. Nanteuil and the Devéria brothers, panels covered with tapestries and drapes with a marked emphasis on red damask. Guigon's logbook makes repeated references to Victor Hugo's set ideas and interference in this domain. His fondness for antiques prompted the following remark by Eugène Mirecourt, a regular visitor to the house : *Victor Hugo is the first to have rekindled our affection for beautiful historic furnishings*[7].

The antechamber (see plan n° 1) had a limestone floor and contained two large wooden chests. Light filtered through the small corner window still in existence today. A large number of pictures, about 80 in December 1840 according to Guigon, lined the walls, including paintings, engravings and plasters as well as *8 large medallions in citrus wood with a large, heavy copper medallion* hung by Guigon in January 1840. In December 1840, a mahogany console was placed between the doors of the kitchen and leather dining-room to display the silverware.

The antechamber adjoined the room known as the leather drawing-room, which was turned into a dining-room (n° 2) in November 1840. Patent leather lined the walls. The flagged limestone and black marble floor, which measured approximately 30 m², was covered over in December 1840 with a rather worn ancient Persian carpet on a red background, bought by Victor Hugo. The latter attentively followed the laying of the carpet, no easy task. Between the windows was a stove draped in a tapestry and *a large carved mediaeval wardrobe dresser*[8]. Opposite this was a straight-backed bench in similar style and between the doors leading respectively to the drawing-room and corridor was a shelf in the same style again. The furniture contained various objects, vases and china. One wall was covered from top to bottom with a vast mediaeval tapestry about four meters wide. A whole panoply of arms was also on display. Hangings in red silk damask masked the doors. The effect was completed in 1837 by a red silk damask ceiling.

The drawing-room (n° 4), situated in the present-day Chinese drawing-room, had, then as now, two windows overlooking the place Royale. The room led into the corridor through a double swing door, walled up in November 1840. A huge carpet covered the 46 m² parquet floor. The walls were covered in red silk damask.

**Layout of the museum**

SECOND FLOOR OF THE MUSEUM

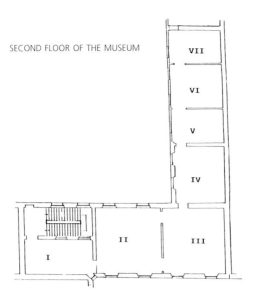

VICTOR HUGO'S APARTMENT

1. Antechamber
2. Leather drawing-room, later leather dining-room (from end 1840)
3. Dining-room until November 1840, then Mme Hugo's bedroom
4. Drawing-room
5. Corridor
6. Bedroom belonging to Mme Hugo until November 1840, Léopoldine until February 1843 and then Adèle
7. Bedroom belonging to Léopoldine until November 1840, then to her brothers
8. Dressing-room
9. Victor Hugo's study
10. Victor Hugo's bedroom
11. Kitchen

f Fireplace
s Stove
--- Presumed location of a door

The windows had matching curtains and blinds as well as white muslin curtains. The room was adorned with a great many drapes and tapestries : a red damask door hanging, over the swing doors leading to the leather dining-room; a silk Chinese-patterned door hanging, covering a large wardrobe door between the mantelpiece and left-hand window; voluminous drapes with silk and gold brocade against a red background, over a wardrobe door to the left of the mantelpiece; *silk drapes with a light blue background and very delicate silk embroidery* over the door leading to the corridor. A tapestry hung on the wall. On the far wall, the fireplace was covered with a gold-studded tapestry. The furniture in this room included gilt consoles, a carved wooden divan and a large gilt sofa with *a silk tapestry canopy lined with red silk damask* made from a piece of red material taken from the dey of Algiers' kasbah in 1830 and given to Victor Hugo by artillery lieutenant Eblé, an acquaintance from his schooldays at Louis-Le-Grand. The canopy is now on display in the museum's staircase. Théophile Gautier used to refer to the sofa ironically as the *dais du dey* *, and a very common, though totally unfounded legend claimed that Victor Hugo used to place himself beneath it.

Beneath the poet's marble bust by David d'Angers was a pedestal covered in gold-studded red silk damask, and Mme Hugo's portrait by Louis Boulanger hung above the bust. The portrait of Victor Hugo and his son François-Victor by Auguste de Châtillon also hung in this room, together with the full-length portrait of General Hugo and Edouard Dubufe's painting of Léopoldine. On 4th July 1837, a painting by Saint-Evre depicting *Inez de Castro* was delivered to the house as a gift from the Duke and Duchess of Orléans, coinciding with the publication of *Les Voix intérieures* and following shortly on the celebrations held by the King on 10th June 1837 in Versailles to inaugurate the historical museum commemorating France's glorious

* *Translator's note* : «dais» in French signifies canopy.

achievements. Victor Hugo had been introduced to the Duchess of Orléans on this occasion. The bill for hanging the picture in the drawing-room still exists[10]. The work itself now hangs in the billiard-room of Hauteville House. In return for this gesture, the poet organised a fête in the place Royale on 21st January 1838.

*Evidence of the poet's passion for mediaeval architecture was everywhere apparent. On the wall hung the most beautiful drawings depicting Antwerp cathedral, a distant view of the Strasbourg steeple, a view of part of Paris with the gothic tower of Saint-Jacques de la Boucherie...*[11].

Until November 1840, the room with two casement windows overlooking the courtyard (n° 3), which occupied part of the present red drawing-room, was used as a dining-room. Before the Hugo family moved in, part of the kitchen was situated here. In November 1840, Mme Hugo moved into this room with Adèle, leaving her former room to Léopoldine. The mantelpiece had been decorated by Victor Hugo with historiated earthenware tiles but they had gone out of fashion and were difficult to find. Mme Hugo's bed had a sky canopy and white muslin curtains. Adèle slept on a sofa between the two windows. A green dressing-table and mirror completed the furniture. Also mentioned are *silk curtains with red and green columns serving as a screen*[12] and an overhang on top of the fireplace.

Léopoldine's new bedroom (n° 6), with one casement window over the courtyard and a fireplace, measured 18 m². White muslin curtains hung from the window and bed. Léopoldine brought her writing-table and piano with her in 1840. Following her sister's marriage, Adèle took over this room.

Little is known about the room next door (n° 7), with one casement window overlooking the courtyard. It first belonged to Léopoldine, before being passed on to her brothers in November 1840. It would appear to have communicated with a dressing-room (n° 8). There was parquet and tiling on the floor.

At the far end of the apartment was Victor Hugo's study, (n° 9), with two windows overlooking the courtyard, and his bedroom, (n° 10), with one window and an exit via a small staircase[13]. The floors were respectively of brown tiles and parquet and covered with rugs. The curtains were green and gold. The study was lit by historiated antique stained glass windows. A large tapestry formed an alcove for the poet's bed. The dressing-room doors were draped in damask and the same red fabric lined the walls of the bedroom. In 1838, a damask-framed painting was fitted into the ceiling. It was almost certainly *Le Moine rouge*, a work by Auguste de Châtillon depicting a monk in flamboyant red habit reading the Bible and lying beside a naked woman. In the study, a historiated mirror in carved wood hung over a divan festooned with green damask cushions. The two rooms contained mirrors, a number of valuable objects, vases and books described in the poem *A des oiseaux envolés (Les Voix intérieures XXII)*. On a table in the study, among the books and papers, lay Christopher Columbus' compass bearing the date *1489* and inscription *La Pinta*. Victor Hugo, who frequently wrote standing up, used a high table for this purpose.

Each of these rooms led off a long corridor with windows (n° 5).

The kitchen, (n° 11), which seems to have undergone a number of unspecified alterations, had one casement window. The floor was limestone, and there was a fireplace.

This was Victor Hugo's fifth home since his marriage to Adèle Foucher in October 1822, and he remained here until July 1848. The poet moved innumerable times during his lifetime, but the longest period was spent in this house. Those sixteen years, flanked by two popular uprisings, are redolent with countless memories of his family and private life on the one hand and his society, literary and political occupations on the other.

Victor Hugo had a particularly soft spot for this house. In a joint letter addressed to Louise Bertin on 6th July 1833, he wrote : *I am still suffering a great deal with my eyes, which adjust as best they can to this square, characterised more by red brick than green leaves. And yet despite this it is beautiful, and I love it.*

In 1838, as member of the Committee for the arts and monuments, he vociferously opposed the plan to demolish the fences surrounding the place Royale, which had been there since 1682, but his objections were overruled and the fences changed in 1839. In his account of the attempted uprising by Barbès and Blanqui on 12th and 13th May 1839, he remarked : *I hear a National Guard bemoan the disappearance of the fence they have just wantonly destroyed, the stumps of which are still sprawled over the pavings. (Choses vues)*

Victor Hugo's move to the place Royale occasioned a mixture of reactions, one of which was summed up by Daumier's cartoon. A parody of *Les Burgraves*, written in 1843 with some of the events taking place at n° 6, place Royale, gives rise to this speech by one of the characters :

*Moi, je sais que ce burg, où maintenant nous sommes,*
*Bâti sur un Marais pour de bons gentilshommes,*
*Fut habité longtemps, puis ensuite quitté*
*Par la cour ; - puis enfin l'oubli, la vétusté*
*L'effaçaient, - quand un jour le maître, ce colosse,*
*- Ne trouvant que ce toit assez haut pour la bosse*
*De son front, - sur ces murs roses quoique noircis*
*Fit luire pour jamais le grand numéro six*[14].

It is easy to imagine the everyday life of Victor and Adèle and their four children, Léopoldine, Charles, Victor[15] and Adèle (born in 1824, 1826, 1828 and 1830). There was much letter-writing, not least by Léopoldine, as well as

Honoré Daumier
*Tenants and Landlords*:
«*The lodging is a little on the expensive side, for the place Royale... - a little expensive... a little expensive to be sure... but as I have already told you, from this very window you can see Victor Hugo rising two or three times a week !...*»

household expense accounts and a great many bills. These remarkably detailed documents provide a vast amount of information on their lifestyle, habits and purchases.

Accounts by some of their close friends convey the family scene. Take Antoine Fontaney's diary entry for 13th March 1834 : [...] *Victor goes off to the dining-room to prepare a surprise for the children. At each table setting, he places a trinket, a biscuit and sweets; then in the middle, he conceals beneath a handkerchief that attractive plaything, the laughing Chinaman. Universal glee ensues*[16].

On 9th April 1843, Balzac wrote to Mme Hanska : *Yesterday I dined at the place Royale. Hugo's second daughter is the greatest beauty I have ever set eyes upon*[17].

The children grew up here. Charles and Victor were boarders at a nearby school, the pension Jauffret. Léopoldine was a half-boarder at the *Externat de Jeunes Demoiselles* at n° 16, place Royale, until 1838, when she started having private lessons at home.

On 15th February 1843, a quiet family dinner took place place Royale in honour of Léopoldine's marriage to Charles Vacquerie, Auguste's brother. And it was also here, only a few months later, that the poet was to live through the tragedy of Villequier.

Juliette Drouet is also associated with this house. They had first met in 1833, and in 1836 she moved nearby to the rue Saint-Anastase. On 13th August 1833, she wrote to Victor Hugo of her sadness on leaving his home : *It was indeed good of you to open the doors of your home to me, it implied to me far more than the satisfaction of idle curiosity and I thank you for having revealed the place where you live, love and reflect. Yet to be honest with you, my beloved, I must confess that I brought back with me a sense of sadness and deep discouragement. I am now far more aware of the abyss which separates us and the extent to which I am alien to you.*

The salons of the place Royale played host to all the celebrities of the day, as corroborated by the following accounts :

*Familiar faces from rue Notre-Dame-des-Champs days [...] were joined in the artistic gatherings of the place Royale by a whole host of new friends. All the latest names in literature flocked there to pay tribute to the figure they all acclaimed as their leader*[18].

*I often recall those joyful, glorious days when Victor Hugo still lived in his magnificent apartment in the place Royale, filled with historic souvenirs, in which we whiled away so many pleasant evenings*[19].

*It was particularly attractive in summertime; the door of the apartment remained wide open, and the perfume from the flowers and greenery outside wafted in through the windows; the receptions took peace not only in the salons but in the place Royale itself [...]*[20].

*The entire universe of literature, eloquence and politics passed through those rooms. Every ray, spark or glow-worm which flickered under the July government shed its light or lost its phosphorus in those gatherings*[21].

Victor Hugo received Théophile Gautier, Musset, Balzac, Vigny, Gérard de Nerval, Lamartine, Sainte-Beuve, Dumas, Mérimée, Béranger, Charles Nodier, Alphonse Karr, Delphine de Girardin, Berlioz, Liszt, Rossini, the Devéria brothers, Célestin Nanteuil, Louis Boulanger, Tony Johannot, Auguste de Châtillon, Chassériau, David d'Angers, Jehan du Seigneur...

This period saw the banning of *Le Roi s'amuse* (1832) and the creation of a number of major dramatic works such as *Marie Tudor* (1833), *Angelo, tyran de Padoue* (1835), *Ruy Blas* (1838), *Les Burgraves* (1843), *Claude Gueux* (1834), *Les Chants du crépuscule* (1835), *Les Voix intérieures* (1837), *Les Rayons et les Ombres* (1840), *Le Rhin*, a significant part of *Les Misérables*, under its initial title *Les Misères*, the beginning of *La Légende des siècles* and *Les Contemplations*.

In 1841, after four unsuccessful attempts (in 1836, 1839 and 1840), the poet was admitted to the Académie française, where he took over from Népomucène Lemercier.

This opened up the doors to a political career. On 13th April 1845, Louis-Philippe appointed Victor Hugo peer of France. During the February 1848 uprisings, in defence to his oath, he made stirring speeches in the place de la Bastille and place Royale, in a vain attempt to sway the people in favour of a regency led by the Duchess of Orléans. On 2nd March, he was involved in planting a tree of liberty in the place des Vosges.

Herman Vogel
*Réception de Victor Hugo à l'Académie française le 3 juin 1841*

Elected deputy for Paris in June 1848, he gave his first speech before the Constituent Assembly on 20th of that month, in favour of reforming the national workshops. On 24th June, the place Royale did not escape the repercussions of the workers' revolt. In *Choses vues*, Victor Hugo describes how a representative, M. Bolley, met him on his return to the Assembly after visiting a barricade place Baudoyer, to tell him that his house in the place Royale had been set on fire. His family had found shelter in the house of the heating caretaker, Martignoni[22].

Luckily, the information proved to be groundless, but the apartment belonging to the former peer had been ransacked. Victor Hugo described the incident at length and in detail many years later. The rioters entered via the impasse Guéménée. *As they entered the courtyard, one of them cried «This is the home of the peer of France !» And immediately word spread among the terrified neighbours* : n° 6 is about to be looted !

They entered the deserted apartment and found their way to the poet's study. *Everything was scattered around, in that state of mild untidiness which indicates that work is in progress.*

This account, which was written after the event, stresses the care and silence of the rioters as they went about their task, respectful of the property of the peer of France. *Once they had gone, and the apartment was empty, we realised that their bare feet had not defiled anything and that their hands, blackened with powder, had touched nothing. Not a single valuable item was missing, not one paper had been displaced.* (*Actes et Paroles - Depuis l'exil*)

This version coincides with the one contained in a letter from Victor Hugo to Alphonse Karr on 3rd July 1848 : *My dear friend, you have doubtless read of the invasion of my house by rioters, but I owe it to them, and readily acknowledge, that they did not disturb a single thing : they left as they had entered. All that was missing was a file of petitions I had left on a table in my study* […].

Herman Vogel
*Victor Hugo plantant l'arbre de la Liberté place Royale le 2 mars 1848*

It must nevertheless be said that these were violent days. On 25th June, Victor Hugo wrote : *My gateway has been hit by fourteen bullets, eleven on the outside and three within. A line soldier was killed in my own courtyard. There are still traces of blood on the cobblestones. (Choses vues)*

Traumatised by all these events, the family left the place Royale on 1st July 1848, moving first to 5, rue de l'Isly, and, in October of that same year, to 37, rue de la Tour-d'Auvergne.

Frédéric-Théodore Lix
*Envahissement de l'appartement de Victor Hugo par les émeutiers le 24 juin 1848*

1. The square known initially as the *place Royale* changed its name on several occasions. During the Revolution, it became the *place des Fédérés*, followed by the *place de l'Indivisibilité*, before adopting the name *place des Vosges* in 1800 as a tribute to the first department to settle its taxes. Under the Restoration, it was renamed *place Royale*, in 1848 went back to *place des Vosges*, became *place Royale* once more under the Second Empire before finally being called *place des Vosges* in 1872, the name it has retained to this day.
2. Letter conserved at the Maison de Victor Hugo.
3. F.-V. HUGO, «Le Marais et la Place Royale», *Paris Guide par les principaux écrivains et artistes de la France*, part 2, Paris, 1867, p. 1321-1337.
4. V.-P. BOTKINE, *Un Russe à Paris*, quoted in «V.-P. Botkine chez Victor Hugo», *Revue de littérature comparée*, vol. 154, April-June 1965, p. 287-290.
5. «Victor Hugo à la place Royale», *L'Amateur d'autographes*, 15th July 1903.
6. L. ARNOULD, «Une soirée chez Victor Hugo le 27 septembre 1846», *Les Annales Romantiques*, vol.III, Geneva, 1967, pp. 149-177.
7. E. de MIRECOURT, *Victor Hugo*, Paris, 1856, p. 25.
8. Guigon's logbook.
9. *Ibid*.
10. Logbook kept by the upholsterer Preux in 1837 and 1838. Maison de Victor Hugo.
11. V.-P. BOTKINE, *op. cit.*
12. Guigon's logbook.
13. The layout given here contradicts some accounts which place the poet's study at the far end of the apartment. Our hypothesis is based on an examination of the logbook kept by the polisher Guigon.
14. *Les Barbus-graves. Parodie des Burgraves de M. Victor Hugo*, by M. Paul ZERO, 1843.
15. Victor only adopted the name François-Victor in 1849, when he began contributing to *L'Evénement*, in order to distinguish himself from his father.
16. A. FONTANEY, *Journal intime*, Paris, 1925.
17. H. de BALZAC, *Lettres à Madame Hanska*, 1832-1844, Paris, 1990.
18. E. de MIRECOURT, *op. cit.*
19. Th. Pavie, quoted by A. PAVIE, *Médaillons romantiques*, Paris, 1909, p. 58.
20. Th. de BANVILLE, *Mes souvenirs*, Paris, 1882.
21. L. ULBACH, *Nos contemporains*, Paris, 1883.
22. La Maison de Victor Hugo still has a number of bills from Martignoni, the heating caretaker from n° 10, place Royale, who worked in the apartment.

## Tour summary

The second floor of the museum was entirely rearranged in 1983, and only gives a vague idea of the apartment as it was in Victor Hugo's day. As for the original plan, as we have seen it was totally altered. Furthermore, very few mementoes from this period have been handed down to us.

The poet, who had taken refuge in Brussels on 12th December 1851, had his assets auctioned in his apartment at 37, rue de la Tour-d'Auvergne, on 8th and 9th June 1852. Afraid the goods might be confiscated by the political regime then in power, Victor Hugo had worked out the details of the auction with Adèle. Théophile Gautier and Jules Janin, out of solidarity with their exiled friend, gave the event a great deal of press coverage, and a large crowd turned up, but the auction only fetched 14 000 F. Théophile Gautier concluded his article in *La Presse*, on 7th June 1852, in these terms : *Let us hope that the poet's many admirers will flock to this unfortunate sale, which they should have prevented, buying the house and the furniture it contains by subscription in order to return them to their mentor at some later date or else to France if he fails to come back. In any event, let them not forget that these are not items of furniture they are buying, but relics.*

A number of items and souvenirs not included in the auction found their way into Victor Hugo's exile. Others were bought by friends, in particular Paul Meurice, who gave great support to Adèle Hugo during this period. The sale catalogue, merely an imprecise list of furniture and objects, some of which belonged in the place Royale before being removed to the rue de la Tour-d'Auvergne, does not allow many links to be established with objects already known to us or others which might one day turn up, so little insight is gained from it. In such a context, the recent acquisition by the museum of a writing case which once belonged to Victor Hugo (displayed in room II), authenticated by a certificate drawn up by the expert in charge of the 1852 auction, is no mean feat.

The chronological approach adopted in the presentation of the rooms allows the place Royale period to come alive.

**ROOM I**

The first room depicts the family, Victor Hugo's ancestors and relatives, his childhood and youth, engagement and marriage to Adèle Foucher, and the birth of their children, right up until they moved to the place Royale.

Victor Hugo's maternal grandparents were from the Nantes region : Jean-François Trébuchet (1731-1783), a sea captain who played a part in the slave trade, shown here holding an octant, and his wife, Renée-Louise née Le Normand (1748-1780). One of their daughters, Sophie, was born in 1772, and in 1797 married Léopold Hugo.

The latter (1773-1828), of Lorraine stock and a fervent Republican, had been sent by the Convention to quell the Vendée movement. There are several portraits of him here, including the one in general's uniform, by Julie Duvidal de Montferrier, in which he appears with his brothers Louis and François and his son Abel, Victor Hugo's elder brother. The two travel chests displayed here almost certainly belonged to him.

Anon.
*Sophie Trébuchet*

Achille Devéria
*Victor Hugo*
*en 1829*

They are covered in leather and studded with nails spelling out *1684* and *1731* respectively.

Three sons were born to Léopold Hugo and Sophie Trébuchet : Abel on 15th November 1798, Eugène on 16th September 1800 and Victor on 26th February 1802 in Besançon, where his father was stationed (Hubert Clerget. *Maison natale de Victor Hugo à Besançon*).

Victor Hugo's childhood was haunted by the memory of the garden at Les Feuillantines, the house he and his brothers shared with their mother, separated from her husband, between 1809 and 1813.

*J'eus dans ma blonde enfance, hélas ! trop éphémère,*
*Trois maîtres : - un jardin, un vieux prêtre et ma mère.*
*Le jardin était grand, profond, mystérieux,*
*Fermé par de hauts murs aux regards curieux,*
*Semé de fleurs s'ouvrant ainsi que des paupières,*
*Et d'insectes vermeils qui couraient sur les pierres ;*
*Plein de bourdonnements et de confuses voix ;*
*Au milieu, presque un champ, dans le fond, presque un bois.*
(*Les Rayons et les Ombres*, XIX)

In March 1811, mother and children left Paris for Madrid, where they were to join Léopold, now a general. The journey, in convoy, in a large carriage with an escort to protect them from the dangers of highway travel, was to remain with Victor Hugo forever (Jules Garnier. *Le Voyage en Espagne*). Once in Madrid, Eugène and Victor became boarders at the Nobles college for a few months, before returning to Paris with their mother, leaving Abel in Spain with his father.

Achille Devéria
*Adèle Hugo*
Circa 1824

Achille Devéria
*Adèle Hugo*
Circa 1827

These years are also associated with the young poet's growing love for Adèle Foucher, a childhood friend and the daughter of Pierre Foucher, head of recruitment at the War Ministry (*Portrait de Pierre Foucher* by Auguste de Châtillon, 1836; *Portrait de Mme. Foucher* (1779-1827) by Achille Devéria). Adèle herself was a talented artist, as can be seen as early as 1820 in her self-portrait and the drawing she made of Victor Hugo.

In 1822, Victor Hugo went to stay at Gentilly, where the Fouchers had rented a house for the summer. Louis Boulanger's drawing shows the spot where Victor, now engaged to Adèle, stayed, with a room in the dovecote. Below the picture are two handwritten lines of verse

*Vallon ! j'ai bien souvent laissé dans ta prairie,*
*Comme une eau murmurante, errer ma rêverie;*
(*Odes*, V,X)
and another handwritten note :
*Ce dessin représente la tour que j'habitais en 1822 et 1823, près du clocher de Gentilly, et m'a été donné par Boulanger, le jour de ma fête, 21 juillet 1832.*

On 12th October 1822, the couple were married in the church of Saint-Sulpice. Victor and Adèle moved in with Adèle's parents, who lived in the Hôtel de Toulouse, headquarters of the council of war, in the rue du Cherche-Midi (see drawing by L. Le Rivercad), until June 1824, when they settled rue de Vaugirard, where Léopoldine and Charles were born. In April 1827, they moved to a house surrounded by gardens in the rue Notre-Dame-des-Champs (see drawing by Jean Coraboeuf). The house, which disappeared when the boulevard Raspail was opened up, became a favourite haunt for Romantic artists such as Sainte-Beuve, Eugène and Achille Devéria and Louis Boulanger, who lived in the same street. Victor Hugo's second son, Victor, was born here. The furore surrounding the first performances of *Hernani* prompted their landlord to evict the family, however, and in May 1830 they moved to the rue Jean Goujon where Adèle was born soon afterwards, and from there to the place Royale. The drawings displayed in this room, by the Devéria brothers, who had got to know Victor Hugo in December 1824, and Louis Boulanger, capture the poet as family man, surrounded by his wife and young children shortly before moving into the place Royale.

Also in this room is the portrait by Baron Gérard of Julie Duvidal de Montferrier, one of his pupils. She gave drawing lessons to Adèle Foucher and married Abel Foucher in 1827.

Finally one comes to a series of cartoons of Paul Foucher, Adèle's younger brother and a friend of Victor's, drawn by his former schoolfriend Alfred de Musset, who was 18 in 1828. Musset had been introduced into the literary circle. He depicts his friend looking at the theatre column during the performance of *Amy Robsart*. Victor Hugo put on the play at the Odéon theatre, under the name of his young brother-in-law. The play was inspired by Sir Walter Scott's *Kenilworth Castle*, and the costumes designed by Delacroix. The work was so disastrously received that it only lasted for one performance, on 13th February 1828.

Anon.
*Jean-François Trébuchet*

Anon.
*Renée-Louise Trébuchet*

Julie Duvidal de Montferrier
*Le Général Léopold Hugo avec deux de ses frères et son fils Abel*

Louis Boulanger
*Gentilly*
Circa 1829

**ROOM II**

This second room recreates as accurately as possible the atmosphere of the drawing-room in the place Royale, which used to be situated where the Chinese drawing-room is today. The damask-draped walls, gilt consoles and Venetian mirror reflect the decoration of the time; several of the paintings used to hang in Victor Hugo's drawing-room, such as the full-length portrait of General Hugo, Louis Boulanger's painting of Mme Hugo (presented at the 1839 Salon) and the one of Victor Hugo and his son Victor by Auguste de Châtillon (1836 Salon). The large earthenware pot in the background illustrates the poet's fondness for Far-Eastern pottery. The painting was to hang later in the billiard-room at Hauteville House in Guernsey, where it has now been replaced by a copy.

Another portrait of Victor Hugo's second son, painted in 1834 by Charles de Champmartin, is on show in this room.

David d'Angers' bust of the poet was given pride of place in the place Royale drawing-room. Victor Hugo met the sculptor in May 1827. He dedicated one of the pieces in *Les Feuilles d'automne* to the artist, on 28th July 1828 (*A M. David, statuaire*, VIII) and another piece, dated April 1840, published in *Les Rayons et les Ombres* (*Au statuaire David*, XX). The marble bust, bearing the artist's dedication and signature, is dated 1838. In a letter dated 21st May of the same year, preserved in the Maison de Victor Hugo, the poet wrote to the sculptor : *In the most magnificent guise, my friend, it is immortality that you have sent me. One can never repay such a debt; I will attempt, however, if not to repay it, at least to recognise its worth.*

Louis Boulanger's *Le Feu du ciel* was also placed in the Hugo family's drawing-room. In this vast contemporary composition, the painter illustrated the

David d'Angers
*Buste de Victor Hugo*
1838

Auguste de Châtillon
*Victor Hugo et son fils Victor*
1836

Louis Boulanger
*Adèle Hugo*
(1839 Salon)

poem entitled *Les Orientales*, dated October 1828, depicting the violence of the divine wrath which brought about the destruction of Sodom and Gomorrha. The writer and artist's mutual affection is apparent from their correspondence as well as in the dedications to some of the poems.

Prominence is given here to the memory of Léopoldine, Victor Hugo's elder daughter, who died tragically on 4th September 1843, at the age of nineteen, in a drowning accident near Villequier, with her husband Charles Vacquerie, only a few months after their wedding. Louis Boulanger's portrait shows her at the age of four. Several of Mme Hugo's drawings depict Léopoldine. On one of them, the four children are indicated by their nicknames : *Didine, Charlot, Toto, Dédé*. The last two portraits are signed and dated *1833*.

Inserted into Mme Hugo's portrait of her daughter reading, signed and dated *avril 1837*, is a small piece of fabric from the dress she wore in Auguste de Châtillon's painting, *Léopoldine au livre d'heures*. Victor Hugo later labelled it *Robe de Didine. 1834. V.H.* and added these two lines :

*Oh ! la belle petite robe*
*Qu'elle avait, vous rappelez-vous ?*
(*Les Contemplations*, IV, VI)

He framed the entire composition himself in the studded red velvet he used for several other works, such as Léopoldine's portrait by Edouard Dubufe, which also hung in the drawing-room of the place Royale.

Auguste de Châtillon, a family friend, painted the portrait *Léopoldine au livre d'heures* in 1835. On the top right appear the dates *28 août 1824* (Léopoldine's date of birth) and *28 août 1835* (probably the date of completion). Léopoldine is holding a book of hours, open at a page decorated with a miniature showing the Dormition of the Virgin Mary. The following verses from *A des oiseaux envolés* may well refer to this work :

*Je vous laisserai même, et gaîment, et sans crainte,*
*O prodige ! en vos mains tenir ma bible peinte,*
*Que vous n'avez touchée qu'avec terreur,*
*Où l'on voit Dieu le père en habit d'empereur !*
*(Les Voix intérieures, XXII)*

It was in 1835 that Léopoldine first started attending catechism classes to prepare for her First Communion, which took place on 8th September 1836 in the church at Fourqueux, where Victor Hugo had sent the family for the summer. All her nearest and dearest were there, most notably her grandfather Pierre Foucher, Théophile Gautier and Auguste de Châtillon, who captured the scene in a painting. Victor Hugo can be seen on the right, head bent. The picture was presented at the 1837 Salon. It remained in the family, and during the period of exile hung in Mme Hugo's bedroom in Hauteville House. It was included in the bequest made by the family in 1927 of their Guernsey home.

One can still see objects belonging to Léopoldine, such as her cashmere shawl, kid gloves and pouch, napkin ring marked *Didine*, small ointment box and embroidered velvet needlecase, a reminder of the considerable importance given to sewing and embroidery work in the education of the time.

In this room, next to Louis Boulanger's picture, are several portraits of Mme Hugo, including a self-portrait in graphite and pastels and the plaster bust made by Victor Vilain and dated 1847.

The memory of Juliette Drouet (1806-1883) is also

Adèle Hugo
*Léopoldine lisant*
1837

Auguste de Châtillon
*Léopoldine au livre d'heures*

evoked here. Victor Hugo first met her in February 1833. She was still an actress at the time, and playing the rôle of Princess Negroni in *Lucrèce Borgia* at the Théâtre de la Porte-Saint-Martin. A portrait of Victor Hugo by Louis Boulanger gives a good idea of his appearance at that period of his life. One can see the insignia he wore as chevalier de la Légion d'Honneur, an award granted to him, as well as to Lamartine, in 1825, when he was only 23, by Charles X. Only a few documents showing Juliette as a young woman have survived. One of these is the picture by Charles de Champmartin (circa 1827) and Léon Noël's lithograph (1832).

It is worth pausing a moment to examine Victor Hugo's own drawing, in brown ink and graphite, of his coat of arms. The latter was adopted by him in 1845, upon becoming a peer, and is made up on the left of the arms of the Hugo de Lorraine family, from which he believed he descended, and on the right of those of his father, who had risen to the rank of Count under the Empire following his victory over a Spanish guerilla leader at Sigüenza, in July 1810. The coat of arms, topped by a helmet and Count's crown, is outlined against the coat of peer of France, itself topped by a Viscount's crown. In 1828, following General Hugo's death, Abel became Count, Eugène Viscount and Victor Baron. In 1837, on his brother Eugène's death, the title of Viscount was handed down to Victor.

In a corner of the room is a wooden chest bearing the initials of the poet's second son, François-Victor, who changed his name in 1849, when working on the paper *L'Evénement*, in order to avoid confusion with his father. This object, engraved and painted by Victor Hugo, gives a foretaste of one of the facets of the poet's personality, that of draughtsman and decorator. Legend has it that when Louis Napoléon Bonaparte called on Victor Hugo in the rue de la Tour-d'Auvergne in October 1848 to ask for his support as presidential candidate, he was seated next to his host on this very chest.

The lacquered dressing-table comes from Mme Hugo's bedroom in Hauteville House.

Adèle Hugo
*Léopoldine,
Charles,
Victor et
Adèle*
1833

**ROOMS III AND IV**

The Chinese drawing-room and the adjoining room lead the visitor into the period of exile.

Following Louis Napoléon Bonaparte's coup d'Etat, Victor Hugo left France for Brussels under a false passport. He spent several months in Belgium before setting off for Jersey. He arrived on 5th August 1852 and the family remained there until October 1855, the beginning of their long sojourn in Guernsey.

On 9th November 1855, they set up home in a furnished house, at n° 20, rue de Hauteville. On 16th May 1856, the poet acquired n° 38, Hauteville House and in November 1856 the family moved in.

Juliette Drouet, who had also gone into exile, set up home at La Fallue on 19th December 1857. Her house was so close to Hauteville House that she could see Victor Hugo's window from there. She left on 15th June 1864, moving to n° 20, rue de Hauteville, the very house in which the Hugo family had spent their first year in exile.

Anon.
*Juliette Drouet*

Juliette Drouet's drawing-room at Hauteville Fairy

Juliette's new house, christened Hauteville Fairy, was a joint purchase by Victor Hugo and Juliette Drouet, with the latter as usufructuary. The magnificent decor designed by the poet for this house was later recreated for the inauguration of the museum in the place des Vosges.

The only documents showing the original layout are the photographs on display in room IV, and these show quite clearly that the panels of the Chinese drawing-room were used to decorate two rooms, Juliette Drouet's drawing-room and bedroom. The difficulties inherent in transposing such a decor to a differently-proportioned room situated in a museum were enormous. Nevertheless, the current presentation, which closely resembles the 1903 version, is a faithful rendition of the atmosphere of Juliette Drouet's home and the spirit of its creator.

Victor Hugo's aptitude for interior decoration and drawing was given free rein at Hauteville House. The Bibliothèque Nationale owns an exercise book containing several preparatory sketches for the work, which was engraved and painted on to wooden plates by Victor Hugo. A pre-exile example of this technique is demonstrated in the chest shown in the previous room, bearing François-Victor's initials, and was to be much used at Hauteville House.

Decorating began at the end of June 1863, and some of the items of furniture were brought over. Juliette Drouet's correspondence gives an insight into the various stages of Victor Hugo's work. On 13th July she wrote : *My dear treasure-hunter, I was sorry not to have time yesterday to tell you how dazzled, delighted and touched I am by all the beautiful, charming and ingenious things you have had done in my new home.* And on 6th August : *I must thank you, my dear little man, for all the wonderful things you are doing for my room, which will*

*not only stun everyone who sees it but will also become as revered and sacred as a temple to me, because your thoughts are given expression everywhere through the divine shape of art.* [...] *This said, I must return once and for all to my admiration for that outstanding room which is in itself a veritable Chinese ode* [...]. Work continued over the following months. On 9th October Victor Hugo noted in his diary : *I went to n° 20 with JJ and showed her the option I have adopted for the painting of her bedroom.* On 2nd March 1864, Juliette wrote to Victor Hugo : *I felt deprived at not being able to go with you and see the wonderful work you continue to carry out on our house.*

The decorator-poet's signature has been apposed in various places. The initials *V H* stand out clearly on the black background surrounding the fireplace and are to be found again on the lower section of a number of panels. A more stylised version serves to decorate the central section of a plaque placed beneath the cornice, to the left of the passageway leading to room IV. And the shadow cast by the little figure on a chair trying to balance on his hands gives a humorous slant to the outline of the *V* and *H*.

The arms of the Lorraine Hugos and those of the General also turn up again in this room.

Allusions to Juliette also appear, although they are not immediately apparent. To the right of the passageway leading to room IV, beneath the cornice, are two complementary panels depicting *Laetitia* and *Harmonia*. The trumpet played by the angel musician forms the letters *J* and *D*. The spirit behind this composition recalls the drawings in which Victor Hugo set his imagination to devising puzzles or historiated initials. On the panel above the little Chinese acrobat a *J* and *D* adorn the body of the vase.

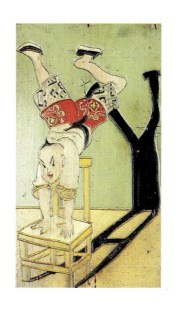

Flowers are prevalent, some of them graced with a butterfly recalling the poem *La pauvre fleur disait au papillon céleste... (Les Chants du Crépuscule,* XXVII).

Several drawings have a humorous note. An anecdote is attached to the portly Chinaman seated before a plate of fish. Following a particularly succulent dish prepared by Suzanne, Juliette's cook, Victor Hugo promised to find her a husband. He therefore devised a character to whom he gave the distorted name *Shu-Zan*. Elsewhere, a parrot is perched on a flower, in a vase; a Chinaman dozes off in his rowing boat; a red-eyed devil sits, arms folded, in an urn; the heart of some of the flowers is decorated with a bird taking flight, a figurine, a pagoda...

The artist's whimsical streak is reflected in two consoles placed between the plate racks, upon each of which are two china figurines. Only the bottom of the clothes belonging to the engraved characters appears, blending into to the black wooden flap. The poet even went as far as to decorate some of the invisible areas on the supports on either side of the fireplace.

The overall effect is completed by some Chinese blinds, purchased in May 1863 according to an entry in Victor Hugo's diary, and the astutely presented crockery, reminiscent of the dining-room decor in Hauteville House. The centrepiece is an opulently decorated fireplace with a Venetian mirror in the middle.

Opposite, above a Chinese cabinet, hangs a mirror framed with a flower and butterfly motif painted by Victor Hugo. The same technique can be found on the first floor of the museum, adorning the frame of the famous *Burg à la Croix*. In the top corners the poet inscribed his initials, offset in gold paint. The family's coat of arms can be seen on one of the downstrokes of the *H*. The mirror is topped with a

wooden band similar to the pier of a fireplace, depicting a Rhineland burg and signed and dated *Victor Hugo 9bre* (November) *1856*. The poet gave the frame to Juliette Drouet on 7th October 1857 to decorate the fireplace in her dining-room.

    Victor Hugo made clever use of all the panels, some of which concealed doors and cupboards, as can be seen from the traces of hinges and locks, to create a kind of jewellery box in order to highlight the numerous items of crockery decorating the racks.

    His taste for antiques and bric-à-brac is well-known. His contemporaries were already struck by this when he lived in the place Royale, but in Guernsey he was able to indulge his hobby even further. The plates are an amalgam of totally different styles, the result of lengthy research by the poet, who never had any qualms about buying up objects in a poor state of disrepair. Several years earlier, when the furniture from the rue de la Tour-d'Auvergne was being auctioned,

Adèle wrote him the following letter, dated 12th June 1852, but her reproach went unheeded : *You have no notion of furnishings. You are forever buying worn fabrics, chipped, cracked or broken china, broken bits of furniture. It costs as much in labour as it would to buy truly valuable objects; if you had bought valuable objects in the first place, you would have received twice what you originally paid for them. [...] my dear, I implore you, please give up all these broken, chipped and torn bits and pieces, and stop believing that every snippet of Lyons cloth is Chinese silk.*

  Juliette Drouet's interior, both in La Fallue and Hauteville Fairy, also contained furniture designed by Victor Hugo. Her bed is missing here but several items, sideboards in particular, which appear on old photographs of her room in Hauteville Fairy, can be seen in room IV. Two of the poet's drawings hang on the wall, and although they are not directly related to the furniture in this room, they illustrate the genesis of his work in this domain. As soon as he moved into Hauteville House, he bought a great number of chests and items in carved wood. He went on to design a collection of totally composite furniture which he had made by a local cabinet-maker called Mauger and his three assistants, who in fact made some of the parts unaided.

  The sideboard on the left is a perfect illustration of this and shows to what extent Victor Hugo allowed his imagination to take precedence over the functional aspect of the furniture. It is made up of a chest decorated with nautical gods, a kind of small tabernacle and a dresser whose two drawers no longer serve any kind of useful purpose. A china bust of Victor Hugo by Louis-Joseph Leboeuf has been placed here. It can also be seen on a photograph of Hauteville Fairy on display in this room. This is a copy of the bust made by the sculptor when staying in Guernsey in April and May 1864.

The large mirrored sideboard was also made from odds and ends. The upper panels are reminiscent of mediaeval carved stalls. They surround an inscription probably added by Victor Hugo, the origins of which are obscure : *20 avril 1843*. A crockery dish decorated with the bust of a man wearing a laurel crown (Petrarch ?) is used, paired with a medallion depicting Victor Hugo, signed and dated *David d'Angers 1828*. As in Hauteville Fairy, the sideboard is adorned with plaster busts by Victor Vilain of Juliette Drouet and her daughter Claire Pradier. Claire, Juliette's daughter by the sculptor James Pradier (1792-1852), was born in 1826 and died in 1846. Victor Hugo linked her memory with that of Léopoldine and devoted several poems from *Les Contemplations* to her.

The third sideboard picks up a number of the floral motifs Hugo frequently used in Hauteville House, carved by Mauger and his workmen. The elements in the centre panels can be linked to the three-feather emblem of Wales. The sideboard is crowned by a figure holding a bird and anchor and the inscription *LUX DUX*. Victor Hugo's coat of arms can also be seen on two of the sideboards.

Victor Hugo added the finishing touches to a bench with the inscription *VIVE AMA*. This takes one back again to Hauteville House, which was full of mottoes, particularly in Latin, which Victor Hugo hoped would be highly instructive.

Between the windows is a folding table designed by the poet. The wooden panel, with antique carved corner pieces, tips over to form the table flap whilst the figure of St. Michael, dated *1652*, pivots on its hinges and drops down to become the table leg.

The same spirit reoccurs in the lantern, embellished with reel-shaped elements.

**ROOM V**

This room is devoted to photography, set in the context of Victor Hugo's exile, during which this recent invention was enthusiastically taken up by the poet's family and friends.

On 5th August 1852, Victor Hugo, accompanied by his son Charles and by Juliette Drouet, landed in Jersey. His wife and daughter were there to greet him, as well as Auguste Vacquerie and a large number of other exiles. On 16th August, the family moved into Marine Terrace, a large whitewashed house on the sea front. Victor Hugo described it in these terms : *A sloping garden measuring a quarter of an arpent was attached to the house, surrounded by walls, interspersed with granite steps and parapets, totally devoid of trees, bare, and richer in stones than in leaves [...]. From the house, one could glimpse to the right of the horizon, on a hill surrounded by a thicket, a tower with a reputation for being haunted; to the left one could see the dick. The dick was a row of large tree trunks leaning against a wall, planted upright in the sand, withered and dry, with knots, ankylosis and knees like a series of tibias. Always ready to make an enigma of daydreams, one mused as to the men who could have left such lofty tibias. [...] A corridor constituted the hall, with a kitchen, greenhouse and farmyard on the ground floor, and a small drawing-room overlooking the empty street and a fairly large, dimly-lit study; on the first and second floors were the bedrooms, clean, cold and furnished with the bare necessities, which had been recently repainted and hung with white curtains. Such was our abode.* (*William Shakespeare*, part 1, book one, chap. I).

This was the background to those first years in exile. Life got itself organised. Victor Hugo discovered the island, the castle at Gros-Nez, of which he made several drawings, and Montorgueil castle. Charles and François-Victor became enthusiastic photographers. They and Auguste Vacquerie were behind the many prints seen here, and Victor Hugo, like the rest of his family, as well as Auguste Vacquerie and Paul Meurice, who came to visit the exiles, complied willingly with the long sittings involved. The still life with the portrait of Victor Hugo illustrates the photographers' experiments with composition.

Thanks to these photographs, we can visualise Victor Hugo's circle of fellow-exiles, banished by the coup d'Etat : General Le Flô (1804-1887), the publisher Pierre-Jules Hetzel (1814-1886), who succeeded in bringing out *Napoléon le Petit* in 1852 and *Châtiments* in 1853, Hennett de Kesler, journalist and man of letters (who died in Guernsey in 1870), Pierre Leroux (1797-1871), Charles Ribeyrolles, journalist and writer (1812-1860) and many more. There were also a number of Hungarian exiles such as Lazare Mezzaros, Count Sandor-Alexandre Teleki and the violinist Remenyi.

The poet's close friends also included Emile Allix, who became his doctor, and his sister Augustine.

In September 1853, Delphine de Girardin, who was spending a few days in Jersey, introduced Victor Hugo to table-turning, a very popular pastime of the day. For the next two years, until October 1855, lengthy spiritualist sessions took place, only ending when Jules Allix, Emile and Augustine's brother, collapsed in a fit of madness. The accounts drawn up of these talking tables relate strange conversations with such differing personalities as Joan of Arc, Shakespeare, Machiavelli, Rousseau, Marat…and Léopoldine Hugo.

In October 1855, *L'Homme*, the Jersey exiles' newspaper, printed in French in St.Helier with Ribeyrolles as editor, published the letter in which Félix Pyat, a French republican refugee in London, openly criticised Queen Victoria's visit to France. The exiles who supported the protest were duly banished from Jersey, and Victor Hugo and his family therefore left for Guernsey on 31st October 1855.

Jersey
studio
*Marine Terrace*

Jersey
studio
*Victor Hugo*

Victor Hugo remained in Guernsey until August 1870. A number of photographs in this room show Hauteville House, a vast three-storied house decorated entirely by its owner between 1856 and 1859.

To the left of these documents is a photograph of Victor Hugo with his family and friends in the garden of Hauteville House. The fountain from the garden of the Hôtel Rohan-Guéménée can be seen.

Every member of the household had an occupation : Charles wrote plays and novels, François-Victor had undertaken a translation of the works of Shakespeare, published between 1859 and 1866, Adèle played the piano and kept a diary, and their mother completed the memoirs entitled *Victor Hugo raconté par un témoin de sa vie*, published in 1863. And yet Victor Hugo often found himself alone in the house. His wife made frequent visits to Paris and Brussels. In 1861, Charles left for Brussels, where he married Alice Lehaene in 1865. François-Victor went to join his mother and brother in Belgium following the death in January 1865 of his Guernsey fiancée, Emily de Putron.

Adèle, the poet's daughter, fell desperately in love with Lieutenant Pinson and her life was to take a tragic turn. On 18th June 1863, she left Hauteville House, never to return, to join Pinson in Halifax, Canada. On 17th October 1863, their marriage was inaccurately announced in *La Gazette de Guernesey*. Adèle, who was deeply disturbed, pursued Pinson relentlessly for the next few years, supported financially by her father. In 1866 she left for Barbados, a small island in the British West Indies, where Pinson's regiment was stationed. She spent several years there, but was brought back to Paris in February 1872 and admitted to a mental hospital in Saint-Mandé,

Anon. *Victor Hugo en famille dans le jardin de Hauteville House*

The table with four inkstards

too late to see her mother, who had died in Brussels in August 1868, or her elder brother Charles, who died in March 1871. François-Victor died in December 1873. Adèle outlived the rest of her family and died in Suresnes in 1915, at the age of 85.

Four terracotta medallions can be seen on the walls, depicting Victor Hugo, his wife Adèle, Charles and François-Victor. Victor Vilain created these in September-October 1860 on a visit to Guernsey.

In front of the window is the table at which Victor Hugo wrote *La Légende des siècles*. He gave the table to Juliette Drouet on 16th August 1859, and his diary entry for that day reads : *gave JJ. the oak table with twined legs from my look out, inscribing it : - I give this table, upon which I wrote la légende des siècles, to Mme J.D. V.H. Guernsey. 16th August 1859.* - The inscription, set within a cartouche, can be seen on the table, written in ink.

In 1860, Mme Hugo organised a charity bazaar in

aid of a crèche for the poor children of Guernsey. She asked Victor Hugo, George Sand, Alexandre Dumas and Alphonse de Lamartine to donate their inkstands. Lamartine also sent a small glass box which had contained a powder for drying the ink and George Sand added a lighter. Everyone wrote a covering handwritten note :

*I did not actually choose this inkstand; I came by it by chance, and used it for several months; as it has been requested for a worthy cause, I am only too happy to donate it.*
*Victor Hugo*
*Hauteville House*
*June 1860*

*I have spent the last two days looking for an inkstand which was not a present from someone too close, and I have not come up with anything at all, apart from a hideous little bit of wood I use on my travels. I find it so ugly that I am adding a small pocket lighter, which is not much better, but which I do use a lot, and as that is what you asked for, at least your good faith is untainted. I was delighted to see you and am now able to tell you directly how fond I am of you. Please convey my gratitude and devotion to your illustrious companion.*
*George Sand*

*I hereby certify that this is the inkstand I have used to write my last fifteen or twenty tomes*
*Paris, 10th April 1860*
*A. Dumas*

*a gift from Lamartine to the master of the quill.*
*Lamartine*

    A table with drawers was made to hold the various objects, but as no buyer was found, Victor Hugo had to purchase it himself. In 1903, Paul Meurice had a surround made and added a base decorated with four chimaera.

**ROOM VI**

On 5th September 1870, following the defeat of Sedan, Victor Hugo returned to France after almost nineteen years in exile. In Paris, he was given a hero's welcome. He stayed first with Paul Meurice at 5, avenue Frochot.

The armistice signed on 28th January 1871 allowed an assembly to be elected, to sit in Bordeaux and undertake peace negociations. Victor Hugo was elected deputy for Paris but was soon disillusioned with the policy adopted and resigned. He was forced to return to Paris on the sudden death of his son Charles in Bordeaux, in March 1871, and had to go on to Brussels to settle the question of inheritance. He was expelled by the Belgian government following his support for the Communards, and went to Luxembourg, staying some time in Vianden.

Victor Hugo then lived in a succession of different homes, spending another year in Guernsey from 1872 to 1873, but in April 1874 he settled into an apartment at 21, rue de Clichy. A large number of illustrious visitors graced the gatherings held by the poet, and the museum has attempted to recreate the atmosphere of the drawing-room at the time. A document from *La Chronique Illustrée* (18th December 1875) shows Schoelcher, Arsène Houssaye, Auguste Vacquerie, Jules Simon, Louis Blanc, Paul de Saint-Victor, Camille Pelletan, Paul Meurice, Théodore de Banville, Léon Gambetta... On the right, sitting between the latter two, is the deputy Edouard Lockroy who was to marry Charles Hugo's widow, Alice, in April 1877. She can be seen on the left with her two children, Georges and Jeanne. Murano's chandelier, which appears on the photograph, has been placed in this room. The elephant on display in the museum, recalling the model for the Bastille fountain referred to in *Les Misérables* (part 4, VI, II) is inexorably linked with the one in the drawing-room rue de Clichy. Georges Hugo described the room as follows : *The room featured objects I had known all my life* [...]. *First, the bronze Chinese elephant bearing a three-tier pagoda* [...].

*Then the gilt wood furniture, covered with white and pink tapestries, ceremoniously placed in a semi-circle around the fireplace; the red and yellow striped drapes; Boulle's clock; and finally the «pouf», given pride of place in the centre of the room, and from which the precious elephant triumphantly emerged, trunk aloft*[1].

In November 1878, Victor Hugo and Juliette Drouet moved into a private mansion overlooking a garden, at 130 avenue d'Eylau (now 124 avenue Victor-Hugo), where he was to remain until his death. The house has since disappeared, but the armchairs and mirror displayed here come from the avenue d'Eylau drawing-room, as shown in a contemporary photograph.

It was here, on 27th February 1881, that Paris came to pay tribute to the author, now in his eighty-fourth year. The event had considerable impact and it was on this occasion that the part of the avenue where Victor Hugo's house was to be found was renamed in his honour, a quite exceptional occurrence for a living person. In May 1885, the name was extended to the part of the avenue leading up to the Arc de Triomphe.

Alice, now remarried, lived next door with her children Georges (1868-1925) and Jeanne (1869-1941). They had come to play an increasingly important rôle in Victor Hugo's life since the death of Charles and then François-Victor in 1873.

In 1877 he published the collection of poems entitled *L'Art d'être grand-père*. To the left of the picture painted by Charles Voillemot in 1879, a montage of several photographs surrounds a late portrait of Victor Hugo : Charles Hugo and his mother Adèle on the top, Jeanne and Georges in the middle, and then Charles, Alice and Victor Hugo with his grandchildren. In 1879, Léon Bonnat made a portrait of Victor Hugo. Paul Meurice asked him to make a copy of this, which is exhibited here. The poet faces the artist, his left arm leaning on a copy of Homer placed on a table.

Arsène Garnier
*Victor Hugo et ses petits-enfants*

Also in this room is a mirror, its frame a typical example of the decorative compositions conceived in the poet's fertile imagination. It has a bird and flower motif and was created in Guernsey shortly before Victor Hugo's return to France. One can still make out the following verse, addressed to Georges :

*Passereaux et rouges-gorges*
*Venez des airs et des eaux,*
*Venez tous faire vos orges,*
*Messieurs les petits oiseaux,*
*Chez Monsieur le petit Georges.*

On the bottom left is written :
*Dessiné le 11 mai 1870 pendant qu'on me juge et condamne à Paris. V.H.*

Following his exile, Victor Hugo returned three times to Guernsey, first in 1872-1873, and then for one week in 1875 and several months in 1878. The photograph of the poet sitting in the red drawing-room was taken during this last visit.

He also stayed a number of times in Veules-les-Roses in Normandy, as a guest of Paul Meurice. The future founder of the place des Vosges museum had had a house built by the sea, with a summerhouse containing a bedroom and study at Victor Hugo's constant disposal. Auguste Vacquerie was

Léon Bonnat
*Victor Hugo*
1879

another frequent visitor. Two photographs on display in this room were taken by André Quinet in September 1882.

Juliette Drouet's presence and loyalty were an integral part of these latter years. She had moved into the house in the avenue d'Eylau and it was here that she died on 11th May 1883. Jules Bastien-Lepage depicted her shortly before her death, emaciated and worn down by her illness. Georges Hugo remembers her thus : *Later I was to become more familiar with the pale figure swathed in white silk headbands, her gentle face an older version of one of Luini's madonnas. She took small steps, leaving a vague aura of verbena behind her. She wore silk dresses in the Romantic style, and a cameo on a slender gold chain swung from her guipure camisoles. She wore blouses with short peplums and pagoda sleeves, and rather low necklines as befitted the coquetry of her age; puffed cuffs of fine batiste covered her wrists, lending the gestures of her stiff fingers some of their erstwhile charm*[2].

During the summer of 1883, Victor Hugo visited Switzerland with Alice and her children. André Quinet took a photograph of him in a carriage during a stopover in Ragatz.

Towards the end of his life, Victor Hugo, who had never owned any of his Parisian homes, decided to have a mansion built on some adjoining land, set between a garden and courtyard, in a style which would remind him of the place Royale, of which he retained fond memories. The architect

Philippe Leidenfrost was appointed to carry out the project, but Victor Hugo's death on 22nd May 1885 prevented its completion.

A number of portraits of the poet in his latter years are on display in this room : the 1878 portrait by Nadar, four photographs taken by Chalot in 1884, placed here in a single frame. An anecdote is attached to these photographs : unable to make Victor Hugo smile, the photographer had the idea of bringing in his little granddaughter Jeanne. At the sight of her, Victor Hugo's face lit up. To the left of the painting by Charles Voillemot is one of the last two photographs of the poet, taken at home on 12th April 1885 by Charles Gallot.

The bronze bust by Auguste Rodin is one of Paul Meurice's many commissions for the opening of the museum. In fact Rodin had got behind with the work, and only a plaster cast was available for the inauguration. He took it back in April 1904 in order to cast the bust in bronze, but it only reached the museum in March 1908. It would appear that this bust was destined as part of the monument to Victor Hugo commissioned from Rodin in 1891 by the State for the Luxembourg gardens. It was actually placed in the gardens of the Palais-Royal, inaugurated in September 1909 and given to the Rodin museum in 1933. Two dry-point etchings by Auguste Rodin correspond to the sketches made by the sculptor in 1883 in the poet's home, despite Victor Hugo's distaste for long sittings. Auguste-Louis Lepère's drawing was made after the bust was created.

Auguste Rodin
*Buste de*
*Victor Hugo*

Charles Gallot
*Victor Hugo*
*le 12 avril 1885*

**ROOM VII**

> His bedroom in the avenue d'Eylau. It was a small room draped in russet-red drapes. The two doors were concealed by wide-pleated curtains. On the ceiling, a tapestry framed in a wide green velvet band. The Louis XIII style bed with twining columns stretched from the far end of the apartment almost to the fireplace; this was a small white marble affair with a scalloped silk overhang, a clock and two chandeliers. A single window opened on to the garden, letting in a violent stream of light which cast a sheen over the large meuble à deux corps in which my grandfather kept his manuscripts. By the window was the high desk at which he wrote standing up, with Whatman paper, a flat Rouen inkstand, a goose quill, blackened with ink right up to the barb, stuck into its narrow neck, and a saucer full of the gold powder he used to dry the lines he had just written. A Louis XV commode with protruding drawers inlaid with flowers served as his dressing-table. Next to the bed, on a carved oak chiffonier, stood a gilt plaster Justice holding his sword in an aloof gesture. A Smyrna rug muffled one's footsteps.

Georges Hugo manages to bring his grandfather back to life through these memoirs[3]. The poet's bedroom, in which he died on 22nd May 1885, was faithfully recreated from this description as well as from reproductions published in the illustrated journals of the day.

Adrien Marie
*Victor Hugo et ses petits-enfants dans la chambre du poète, avenue d'Eylau*

     The gilt plaster Justice mentioned by Georges Hugo is actually a statue of the Republic holding a sword and leaning on a stele, which was executed by Auguste Clésinger in 1878. The sculptor gave it to Victor Hugo as a birthday present on 26th February 1879.

     On the chest of drawers is a Sèvres porcelain vase with a blue background and a motif painted by T. Fragonard to illustrate Jean-François Regnard's *Le Joueur*. On the evening of 25th February 1881, Jules Ferry, acting on behalf of the government in his capacity as President of the Council, presented this gift to Victor Hugo, then entering his eightieth year.

     To the right of the window one can see that the table invented by the poet to enable him to write standing up is in fact made up of two superimposed tables.

1. G. VICTOR-HUGO, *Mon grand-père*, Paris, 1902.
2. *Ibid.*
3. *Ibid.*

Victor Hugo
*Le Phare des Casquets*

## 1st FLOOR

The first room is given over to a rotating exhibition of Victor Hugo's drawings. The museum owns approximately six hundred of these, and their number is constantly increasing thanks to purchases. The total output is considerable, and a huge part is kept in the Bibliothèque Nationale. In his will, dated 31st August 1881, the poet wrote : *I bequeath all my manuscripts and everything I may have written or drawn to the Bibliothèque Nationale de Paris, which will become one day the Library of the United States of Europe.*

Victor Hugo drew all his life, but only regarded this as a hobby. In his *Salon de 1859*, Baudelaire spoke of *that magnificent imagination which pervades Victor Hugo's drawings as mystery pervades the heavens.* In turn, Victor Hugo wrote from Guernsey, on 29th April 1860, to the author of this eulogy : *The page you sent me, dear poet, was indeed beautifully expressed; I am both happy and proud that you should think so much of what I term my pen and ink drawings. I have now added pencil, charcoal, sepia, soot and all sorts of curious mixtures which more or less convey what my eye, and particularly my mind, can see. It is an amusing diversion between two stanzas.*

From 1830 to 1840 he drew a great many meticulously executed cartoons and landscapes in pen and ink.

Following his journey along the Rhine in 1840, his inspiration altered and diversified. The Rhineland burg swathed in a strange, unreal atmosphere and plunged in darkness is a key element in this visionary universe and was soon to lead Victor Hugo to make full use of the effects of charcoal and wash tints.

The year 1850 stands apart in Victor Hugo's drawing career. At the time, his writing was mainly devoted to political speeches and this allowed drawing to take precedence for a few months. This was the year which saw several major compositions, some of which belonged to Paul Meurice and are

Victor Hugo
*Le Burg
à la Croix*

*Paul Meurice dans son cabinet de travail, rue Fortuny*

now kept in the museum. One of these is *Le Burg à la Croix*, in a format not usually employed by Victor Hugo. The drawing is signed and dated in the bottom left-hand corner, VICTOR HUGO 1850. The work was included in the auction held on 8th and 9th June 1852, after the poet's departure for Brussels following the coup d'Etat. It was purchased by Paul Meurice, and one can see the drawing, together with *Le Phare des Casquets* and *Le Phare d'Eddystone*, on a photograph of Paul Meurice taken in his study. On his return to France in 1870, Victor Hugo refused to take back his drawing, embellishing it with an engraved, painted frame, decorated with birds, insects and flowers. It reads *Victor Hugo / Siège de Paris /(5 7bre 1870. 3 février 1871)*. There is a clear analogy between this and some of the pictures designed for Hauteville House or Hauteville Fairy.

During the years of exile, the ocean became a key source of inspiration. The poet's imagination led him to try out new forms of expression such as cut-out stencils enabling parts of the drawing to be reserved, metal lace printing and the deliberate use of stains... He even gave his name a disproportionate amount of space within the framework of the drawing, so that it frequently became an integral part of the whole composition. It was during this period that he made a number of sketches for the interior decoration of Hauteville House.

From the 1860s on, his frequent journeys gave rise to a significant number of travel drawings. The series of drawings associated with *Les Travailleurs de la mer* also belong to this period.

In 1866, while writing *L'Homme qui rit*, Victor Hugo composed *Le Phare des Casquets* and *Le Phare d'Eddystone*, key works in the museum's collection. *In the seventeenth century a lighthouse was a sort of plume of the land on the seashore. The architecture of a lighthouse tower was magnificent and extravagant. It was covered with balconies, balusters, lodges, alcoves, weathercocks. Nothing but masks, statues, foliage, volutes, reliefs, figures large and small, medallions with inscriptions.* Pax in bello, *said the Eddystone lighthouse. [...] Besides whimsical designs in stone, they were loaded with whimsical designs in iron, copper, and wood. The iron-work was in relief, the wood-work stood out. On the sides of the lighthouse there jutted out, clinging to the walls among the arabesques, engines of every description, useful and useless, windlasses, tackles, pulleys, counterpoises, ladders, cranes, grapnels. On the pinnacle around the light, delicately-wrought iron-work held great iron chandeliers, in which were placed pieces of rope steeped in resin; wicks which burned doggedly, and which no wind extinguished; and from top to bottom the tower was covered by a complication of sea standards, banderoles, banners, flags, pennons,*

Victor Hugo
*Le Phare d'Eddystone*

*colours which rose from stage to stage, from story to story, a medley of all hues, all shapes, all heraldic devices, all signals, all confusion, up to the light chamber, making, in the storm, a gay riot of tatters about the blaze.* […]

*It was* [the Casquets lighthouse], *at that period* […] *a flaming pile of wood under an iron trellis, a brazier behind a railing, a head of hair flaming in the wind. (L'Homme qui rit, part 1, II, XI)* \*

The museum collections also include an important series of drawings from Victor Hugo's time in Vianden in 1871.

Towards the end of his life, the poet, true to his principles, demonstrated his opposition to capital punishment in a series of cartoons with the overall title *Le Poëme de la*

\* Translation taken from *The Laughing Man by Victor Hugo. The authorized English translation.* Published by George Routledge & Sons, 1887.

*Sorcière*. Georges Hugo takes up the story once more :
*I sometimes saw him drawing at that time; just small rapid sketches, landscapes, cartoons, profiles captured in a single stroke, made on the first scrap of paper that came to hand. He threw down the ink haphazardly, flattening the goose quill which squeaked and spewed black jets. He then virtually moulded the inkspot, which grew into a burg, forest, fathomless lake or storm-laden sky; he delicately moistened the barb of the quill with his lips, creating a cloudburst to make the rain fall upon the damp drawing; or else he indicated precisely the mists veiling the horizon. He then finished using a wooden matchstick to draw in delicate architectural details, adding flowers to the ogives, making a gargoyle smirk, placing the ruin on a tower, and the match between his fingers became a chisel*[1].

Following this all-too-brief look at Victor Hugo's drawings, rendered necessary by the frequently changing displays in this room, we leave the last word to Théophile Gautier. In an article published in *La Presse* on 7th June 1852, he wrote : *If he were not a poet, Victor Hugo would be a first-class painter; he excels at blending, in the most somber, untamed streaks of fantasy, the clair-obscur effects of Goya with the architectural terror of Piranesi; in the midst of threatening shadows, he manages to outline the towers of a demolished burg in a shaft of moonlight or a clap of thunder and emphasise the black silhouette of a faraway city with its needles, steeples and belfreys in a single livid ray of the setting sun. Many a decorator would envy his strange ability to create dungeons, old streets, castles and ruined churches in such an extraordinary style and with such unfamiliar architecture, brimming with love and mystery yet as oppressive as a nightmare.*

The adjoining rooms are devoted to exhibitions and temporary displays (illustrations of Victor Hugo's works, documents pertaining to his life and family, cartoons...).

1. G. VICTOR-HUGO, op.cit.

**THE STAIRCASE**

The works hanging in the staircase are subject to alteration. Several of them illustrate Victor Hugo's works or events which made a particular impact on his life.

On the ground-floor are the charcoal drawings by Maillart (1840-1926) and Gustave Brion (1824-1877) for *Quatrevingt-treize*.

On the first-floor landing, the panel taken from the dey of Algiers' kasbah in 1830 and presented to Victor Hugo by Lieutenant Eblé used to belong, as we have seen, in the drawing-room of the place Royale.

- Henri Fantin-Latour (1836-1904), *Le Satyre* (*La Légende des siècles*, part 1, VIII) :

*Soudain il se courba sous un flot de clarté,*
*Et le rideau s'étant tout à coup écarté,*
*Dans leur immense joie il vit les dieux terribles.*

- Luc-Olivier Merson (1846-1920), *Une larme pour une goutte d'eau* (*Notre-Dame de Paris*, book VI, chap. 4).

Between the first and second floors stands a large bas-relief in coloured glass paste depicting *L'Apothéose de Victor Hugo*, executed at Paul Meurice's request by Henry Cros (1840-1907). The subject chosen refers to a stanza in the poem *Le Cheval* (*Les Chansons des rues et des bois*) :

*C'était le grand cheval de gloire,*
*Né de la mer comme Astarté,*
*A qui l'Aurore donne à boire*
*Dans les urnes de la clarté.*

In the centre, the poet sits astride Pegasus and gallops towards Dawn, who is proferring the urn of light. On the left, the shadow turns back towards darkness. On the lower part of the picture, the nymph Castalie, the poets' muse, is stretched out between the Rhymes, on her right, and the group of Thought, Pan and Enthusiasm, arms outstretched towards the poet, on her left.

François Pompon
*Cosette*

- Daniel Vierge (1851-1904), *Les Funérailles de Charles Hugo*. The poet's elder son died in Bordeaux on 13th March 1871 and was buried in Paris on 18th June, the day of the Commune uprising. The funeral procession had to cross a city in turmoil on its way to the family vault in Père Lachaise cemetery. Victor Hugo and François-Victor were behind the hearse, and as they proceeded, the troops presented arms. Victor Hugo recalled the day's events in *Choses vues*.

On the second-floor landing, the wood panelled wardrobe door comes from Victor Hugo's room in Paul Meurice's house at Veules-les-Roses, as does the Louis XIII style table on the next landing.

The plaster statue of Cosette is by François Pompon (1855-1933), who presented the work at the 1888 Salon.

- Alexandre Steinlen (1856-1923), *Les Pauvres Gens* (*La Légende des siècles*, part 1, XIII, 3) :
*Tiens, dit-elle en ouvrant les rideaux, les voilà !*

- Eugène Grasset (1845-1917), *Eviradnus*
*La Légende des siècles*, part 1, V, 2) :
*Et, prenant aux talons le cadavre du roi,*
*Il marche à l'empereur qui chancelle d'effroi;*
*Il brandit le roi mort comme une arme, il en joue,*
*Il tient dans ses deux poings les deux pieds, et secoue*
*Au-dessus de sa tête, en murmurant : Tout beau !*
*Cette espèce de fronde horrible du tombeau,*
*Dont le corps est la corde et la tête la pierre.*
*Le cadavre éperdu, se renverse en arrière,*
*Et les bras disloqués font des gestes hideux.*

Albert Besnard
*La Première
d'Hernani*

Victor Hugo's portrait by François-Nicolas Chifflart (1825-1901) was painted in February 1868 during a visit the artist made to Guernsey, and presented at the Salon that same year. Victor Hugo's diary tells us that the sitting took place on 9th February. The initials *F C* appear engraved in the stone upon which the poet is leaning. François-Nicolas Chifflart made a number of illustrations of Victor Hugo's work, in particular *La Mort de Gilliatt (Les Travailleurs de la mer*, part 3, book III, V).

- Alfred Roll (1846-1919), *L'Entrée de Victor Hugo dans sa quatre-vingtième année*. From his window in the avenue d'Eylau, the poet was able to witness the heartfelt acclaim demonstrated by the Parisians.

- Alfred Roll, *La Veillée sous l'Arc de triomphe*. On 31st May 1885, the day before Victor Hugo's funeral, his body lay in state beneath the Arc de Triomphe. Charles Garnier, who was commissioned to create an ephemeral monument, built a gigantic catafalque. A long black crêpe veil covered the left-hand side of the Arc de Triomphe and Falguière's quadriga above. Forty-four candelabras surrounded the place de l'Etoile and burned all night. The cuirassiers held blazing torches. On 1st June, decreed a day of national mourning, the vast funeral procession set off from the Arc de Triomphe and continued down the Champs-Elysées, the boulevards Saint-Germain and Saint-Michel and the rue Soufflot, ending up at the Panthéon. The decree of 26th May 1885, passed the day after Victor Hugo's death, stated that the church of Sainte-Geneviève, which had been reinstated during the Second Empire, was to be deconsecrated once more. In the staircase one can see the famous portrait of Victor Hugo on his deathbed, photographed by Nadar. When the poet died, Nadar, Bonnat, Carjat, Dalou,

Falguière and Glaize were allowed into his bedroom in the avenue d'Eylau.

- Albert Besnard (1849-1934), *La Première d'Hernani*. The picture was commissioned by Paul Meurice, and attempts to recreate the atmosphere of the première, which took place on 25th February 1830. The play was written between 29th August and 24th September 1829, and opened at the Théâtre-Français on 5th October. The evening of 25th February was of capital importance, marking the beginning of the famous *bataille d'Hernani*, in which the over-excited young Romantics challenged the stalwarts of the classical theatre.

The young Théophile Gautier, seen here wearing his famous red waistcoat, led the defenders of the play, which included Louis Boulanger, Gérard de Nerval, Alfred de Musset, Petrus Borel, Célestin Nanteuil, the Devéria brothers, Auguste de Châtillon... The painter shows the theatre as the curtain is about to rise. The two camps are facing one another, the Romantics easily recognisable from their long hair and eccentric dress. In the bottom right-hand corner, the word *Hierro*, which signifies iron in Spanish, reminds one that this word appeared on all the tickets given by the author to his friends.

- Auguste Leroux (1871-1957), *La Confiance du marquis Fabrice* (*La Légende des siècles*, part 1, VII, 3) :
*Le porte-glaive fit, n'étant qu'un misérable,*
*Tomber sur l'enfant mort la tête vénérable.*

*Et voici ce qu'on vit dans ce même instant-là :*

*La tête de Ratbert sur le pavé roula,*
*Hideuse, comme si le même coup d'épée,*
*Frappant deux fois, l'avait avec l'autre coupée.*

*L'horreur fut inouïe; et tous, se retournant,*
*Sur le grand fauteuil d'or du trône rayonnant*
*Aperçurent le corps de l'empereur sans tête,*

*Et son cou d'où sortait, dans un bruit de tempête,*
*Un flot rouge, un sanglot de pourpre, éclaboussant*
*Les convives, le trône et la table, de sang.*

*Alors, dans la clarté d'abîme et de vertige*
*Qui marque le passage énorme d'un prodige,*
*Des deux têtes on vit l'une, celle du roi,*
*Entrer sous terre et fuir dans le gouffre d'effroi*
*Dont l'expiation formidable est la règle,*
*Et l'autre s'envoler avec des ailes d'aigle.*

- Georges Rochegrosse (1859-1938), *Les Burgraves*. The painter chose to depict the scene in which the Emperor Frédéric Barberousse appears. The elderly Job is standing on the steps. Written between 10th September and 19th October 1842 and performed at the Théâtre-Français in March and April 1843, the play was a complete flop and soon became the butt of a series of parodies. In 1902, it was put on at the Comédie-Française to commemorate Victor Hugo's centenary. Mounet-Sully played Job and Mme Segond-Weber Guanhumara. Hanging in the staircase is a pastel by René Gilbert (1858-1914), showing the actress in this rôle.

François-Nicolas Chifflart, *La Conscience* (*La Légende des siècles*, part 1, I, 2) :
*Caïn, ne dormant pas, songeait aux pieds des monts.*
*Ayant levé la tête, au fond des cieux funèbres,*
*Il vit un oeil, tout grand ouvert dans les ténèbres,*
*Et qui le regardait dans l'ombre fixement.*

- François-Nicolas Chifflart, *Le Jour des rois* (*La Légende des Siècles*, part 1, IV, 5) :
*Alors, tragique et se dressant,*
*Le mendiant, tendant ses deux mains décharnées,*
*Montra sa souquenille immonde aux Pyrénées,*
[...].

# Chronology

| | |
|---|---|
| 1802 | Victor Hugo born in Besançon (26th February). |
| 1803 | Adèle Foucher born. Léopold Hugo takes his three sons to Corsica, and then to Elba where Sophie joins them. |
| 1804 | Sophie and her sons return to Paris : rue Neuve-des-Petits-Champs then rue de Clichy. |
| 1806 | Birth of Juliette Gauvain, the future Juliette Drouet. |
| 1807 | Léopold is appointed military commander of the province of Avellino, near Naples. |
| 1808 | Sophie and the children join Léopold in Naples. |
| 1809 | Sophie and the children return to Paris : rue de Clichy, then rue Saint-Jacques, then impasse des Feuillantines. Victor takes lessons with Father La Rivière (until 1815). |
| 1810 | Léopold is made Count of Sigüenza and appointed governor of several Spanish provinces. Lahorie arrested at Les Feuillantines. |
| 1811 | Sophie and the children join Léopold in Madrid. Eugène and Victor become boarders at Nobles college. |
| 1812 | Sophie, Eugène and Victor return to Les Feuillantines. |
| 1813 | Sophie and the children move into the rue des Vieilles-Tuileries. |
| 1815 | Eugène and Victor become boarders at the pension Cordier. Victor begins his *Cahiers de vers français*. |
| 1816 | *La France en deuil. Le Déluge. Irtamène*. Lessons at the lycée Louis-le-Grand. |
| 1817 | Awarded a distinction by the Académie Française for his competition entry, the poem *Du bonheur que procure l'étude dans toutes les situations de la vie*. Victor begins *Athélie* and writes *A.Q.C.H.E.B.* (A quelque chose hasard est bon). |
| 1818 | Léopold and Sophie obtain legal separation. Victor and Eugène move in with their mother, rue des Petits-Augustins. Enrols in the law faculty. First draft of *Bug-Jargal*. |
| 1819 | Obtains Lys d'or (golden lily award) at the Académie des Jeux Floraux de Toulouse for his ode on *Le Rétablissement de la statue de Henri IV*. The *Conservateur littéraire* is founded. |
| 1820 | Granted royal gratuity for his ode on *La Mort du duc de Berry*. Secret correspondence between Victor and Adèle. Mme Hugo and her children move into the rue de Mézières. Ode on *La Naissance du duc de Bordeaux*. |
| 1821 | Victor begins *Haf d'Islande* (published in 1823). Death of Sophie Hugo. Engagement of Victor and Adèle. |

| | |
|---|---|
| 1822 | Victor moves into the rue du Dragon. Awarded royal grant following publication of *Odes et Poésies diverses*. Adèle and Victor married at the church of Saint-Sulpice and set up home at 39, rue du Cherche-Midi. |
| 1823 | Beginning of *La Muse française*. A son, Léopold-Victor, is born, but survives less than three months. |
| 1824 | *Nouvelles Odes*. Move to 90, rue de Vaugirard. Léopoldine born. |
| 1825 | Victor made chevalier de la Légion d'honneur. Travels to Reims for the Anointment of Charles X. Ode on *Le Sacre de Charles X*. Travels in the Alps. |
| 1826 | Publication of the second version of *Bug-Jarga*, and *Odes et Ballades*. Charles born. |
| 1827 | Ode *A la colonne de la place Vendôme*. Move to 11, rue Notre-Dame-des-Champs. Publication of *Cromwell* and its *Préface*. |
| 1828 | Death of General Hugo. *Amy Robsart* flops at the Odéon theatre. Victor born. |
| 1829 | *Les Orientales, Le Dernier Jour d'un condamné*. *Marion de Lorme* banned. |
| 1830 | *Hernani*. Move to 9, rue Jean-Goujon. Adèle born. |
| 1831 | *Notre-Dame de Paris*. Première and publication of *Marion de Lorme*. *Les Feuilles d'automne*. |
| 1832 | Moves to 6, place Royale. Première of *Le Roi s'amuse*. Play banned, publication. |
| 1833 | *Lucrèce Borgia*. Beginning of affair with Juliette Drouet. *Marie Tudor*. |
| 1834 | *Etude sur Mirabeau, Littérature et philosophie mêlées, Claude Gueux*. Beginning of travels with Juliette. |
| 1835 | *Angelo, tyran de Padoue*. Travels to Normandy and Picardy. *Les Chants du crépuscule*. |
| 1836 | Fails to get into the Académie Française. Travels in Brittany and Normandy. *La Esmeralda* flops at the Opéra (words by Victor Hugo, music by Louise Bertin). |
| 1837 | *Les Voix intérieures*. Hugo promoted to rank of officier de la Légion d'honneur. Travels to Belgium and Normandy. |
| 1838 | Travels to Champagne. *Ruy Blas*. |
| 1839 | Travels to Alsace, Switzerland, Provence and Burgundy. Fails again to enter the Académie. |

| | |
|---|---|
| 1840 | Fails yet again to get into the Académie Française. *Les Rayons et les Ombres*. Travels to the Rhine valley. *Le Retour de l'Empereur*. |
| 1841 | Elected to the Académie Française. |
| 1842 | *Le Rhin*. |
| 1843 | Marriage of Léopoldine and Charles Vacquerie. *Les Burgraves*. Travels to Spain and the Pyrenees. Death of Léopoldine and Charles, drowned in the Seine on 4th September. |
| 1845 | Hugo appointed peer of France. Begins writing *Les Miséres*, later to become *Les Misérables*. |
| 1846 | Speech before the Chamber of Peers. |
| 1847 | Speech favourably inclined towards the return of the Bonaparte family to France |
| 1848 | Hugo elected Paris deputy for the Constituent Assembly. Speech on national workshops. Appointed government representative to restore order among the insurrectionists. His apartment broken into. Moves to 5, rue de l'Isly, then to 37, rue de la Tour-d'Auvergne. *L'Evénement* created. Speech on the freedom of the press. |
| 1849 | Hugo elected Paris deputy for the Legislative Assembly. Speech on destitution. President of the Peace Congress. Travels to Normandy. Speech on the Rome expedition. |
| 1850 | Speech on freedom of teaching. Speech in support of universal suffrage. |
| 1851 | Leaves for Brussels. |
| 1852 | Expelled from France by decree. Furniture sold in Paris. *Napoléon-Le-Petit* published in Brussels. Leaves for Jersey. Moves into Marine Terrace. |
| 1853 | Takes up spiritualism. *Châtiments*. |
| 1854 | *Lettre à Lord Palmerston*. Hugo composes some sections of *La Fin de Satan* (published in 1886). |
| 1855 | Hugo composes part of *Dieu* (published in 1891). Expelled from Jersey. Arrives in Guernsey. |
| 1856 | *Les Contemplations*. Buys Hauteville House. |
| 1858 | *La Pitié suprême, L'Ane* (published in 1879 and 1880). |
| 1859 | Refuses amnesty. *La Légende des siècles*. Intervenes in favour of John Brown. |
| 1860 | Takes up *Les Misérables* again (abandoned since 1848). |
| 1861 | Travels to Belgium and Holland. |
| 1862 | *Les Misérables*. Travels to Belgium, Luxembourg and the Rhine. |

| | |
|---|---|
| 1863 | *Victor Hugo raconté par un témoin de sa vie* by Mme Hugo. Travels to Belgium and Germany. |
| 1864 | *William Shakespeare*. Travels in the Ardennes and the Rhineland. |
| 1865 | Spends time in Brussels. Travels to Germany. Marriage of Charles and Alice Lehaene. *Les Chansons des rues et des bois*. |
| 1866 | Drafts *Mille francs de récompense*. *Les Travailleurs de la mer*. Spends time in Brussels. |
| 1867 | Charles' son Georges born, but only lives for one year. Drafts *Mangeront-ils* ? Publication of *Paris Guide* (with an introduction by Victor Hugo). Revival of *Hernani* at the Théâtre-Français. Travels to Zeeland. *La Voix de Guernesey*. |
| 1868 | Charles' second son Georges born. Mme Hugo dies in Brussels. |
| 1869 | *L'Homme qui rit*. *Le Rappel* founded. President of the Peace Congress. Jeanne, Charles' daughter, born. |
| 1870 | Returns to France (5th September). Moves in with Paul Meurice. First French edition of *Châtiments*. |
| 1871 | Elected Paris deputy and joins the Assembly in Bordeaux, but resigns one month later. Death of Charles. Stays in Brussels and then in Vianden. Back in Paris, moves into 66, rue de la Rochefoucauld. |
| 1872 | Revival of *Ruy Blas*. *L'Année terrible*. Spends a year in Guernsey. |
| 1873 | Moves to 55, rue Pigalle. Death of François-Victor. |
| 1874 | *Quatrevingt-treize*. Moves to 21, rue de Clichy. *Mes fils*. |
| 1875 | Spends one week in Guernsey. *Actes et Paroles* I and II (*Avant l'exil - Pendant l'exil*). Literary testament. |
| 1876 | Elected senator. *Actes et Paroles* III (*Depuis l'exil*). |
| 1877 | 2nd series of *La Légende des siècles*, *L'Art d'être grand-père*, *L'Histoire d'un crime* (1st part). |
| 1878 | *L'Histoire d'un crime* (2nd part), *Le Pape*. Spends four months in Guernsey. Moves into 130 avenue d'Eylau. |
| 1879 | *La Pitié suprême*. Stays in Veules-les-Roses and Villequier. |
| 1880 | *Religions et religion*. *L'Ane*. |
| 1881 | Celebration to mark Victor Hugo's eightieth birthday. *Les Quatre vents de l'esprit*. Draws up his will. |
| 1882 | *Torquemada*. Spends time in Veules-les-Roses. |
| 1883 | Death of Juliette Drouet. 3rd series of *La Légende des siècles*. Adds codicil to will. *L'Archipel de la Manche*. |
| 1884 | Travels to Switzerland. |
| 1885 | Death of Victor Hugo (22nd May). State funeral. |

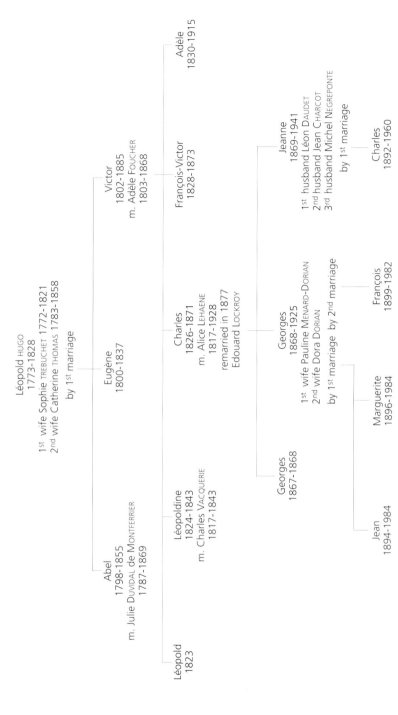

## Practical information

**MUSEUM ENTRANCE**
6, place des Vosges, 75004 Paris

**HOURS OF OPENING**
Tuesday to Sunday
10.00 to 17.40
Closed on Mondays and public holidays
Access to library by appointment only

**TRANSPORT**
Métro Saint-Paul / Bastille / Chemin-Vert
Bus nos 20, 29, 65, 69, 76, 96

**COMMUNICATIONS
AND ACTIVITY CENTRE**
- Groups admitted on request
- Guided tours available on request
  (30 people maximum)
- Information tel. 42 72 10 16

**G**uide written by :
Sophie Grossiord, Curator at the Maison de Victor Hugo

**G**raphic design :
Gilles Beaujard, assisted by Viviane Linois

**P**roduction : Florence Jakubowicz

**E**nglish translation : Caroline Taylor-Bouché

**P**hotoengraving : Bussière Arts graphiques, Paris

**F**lashing : Delta +, Levallois-Perret

**P**rinting : Imprimerie Alençonnaise, Paris

**F**irst printed by imprimerie Alençonnaise in Alençon, February 1993

**I**ndividual orders by minitel (France) : 3615 CAPITALE

**C**over :
Auguste de Châtillon, *Victor Hugo et son fils Victor*, 1836

© Paris-Musées, 1993
Registration of copyright February 1993
ISBN 2-87900-107-2

**P**hotographic acknowledgments :
Photothèque des musées de la Ville de Paris, © by SPADEM 1993 :
I. Andréani, O. Habouzit, Ph. Ladet, D. Lifermann, P. Pierrain, M. Toumazet, J.-Y. Trocaz.
© DAC-DAP, 1993 : Christophe Walter
R.M.N.